RULES AND ADVICE FOR WRITING FICTION AND CREATIVE NONFICTION

THE CREATIVE WRITER'S
style Guide

CHRISTOPHER T. LELAND

WRITER'S DIGEST BOOKS
CINCINNATI, OHIO
www.writersdigestbooks.com

Visit our Web site at www.writersdigest.com for information on more resources for writers.

To receive a free weekly e-mail newsletter delivering tips and updates about writing and about Writer's Digest products, register directly at our Web site at http://newsletters.fwpublications .com.

06   05   04   03   02   5   4   3   2   1

Library of Congress Cataloging-in-Publication Data

Leland, Christopher T.
    The creative writer's style guide: rules and advice for writing fiction and creative nonfiction / by Christopher T. Leland.—1st ed.
        p.   cm.
    Includes index.
    ISBN 1-884910-55-6 (alk. paper)
    1. English language—Rhetoric—Handbooks, manuals, etc. 2. Creative writing—Handbooks, manuals, etc. I. Title.
PE1408.L4124   2002
808'.042—dc21   2002069045
                                                                   CIP

Edited by Donya Dickerson and Jack Heffron
Designed by Sandy Kent
Cover designed by Matthew DeRhodes
Cover photography by Al Parrish
Production coordinated by Kristen Heller

DEDICATION

For my students who for a quarter century have shown me that our stories are perhaps the greatest gift we can render to the world.

ACKNOWLEDGMENTS

Thanks go to The Humanities Center of Wayne State University and its director, Dr. Walter Edwards, under the auspices of which part of this book was written.

To Gesa Kirsch, Pietr Tiersma, Stephenie Steele, and Angie Philpott I owe a great debt for their expert advice regarding certain issues of grammar and usage.

I would also like to acknowledge the efforts of Mitchell Waters, my agent, of Jack Heffron, who launched this project at Writer's Digest Books, and of Donya Dickerson, who saw it to completion.

Finally, as ever, I express my gratitude to my partner, Osvaldo Sabino, whose love and patience in good times and bad have sustained me for twenty-three years.

ABOUT THE AUTHOR

Christopher T. Leland is the author of five novels as well as volumes of literary criticism and translation. In 1998, he published *The Art of Compelling Fiction: How to Write a Page-Turner.* He has taught creative writing courses since 1976 at the University of California, San Diego; Pomona College; Harvard University; and Bennington College. He is presently a professor of English at Wayne State University in Detroit, Michigan.

TABLE *of* CONTENTS

Why Do You Need This Book?

D oes the world really need another manual of style?
Well. . . . Yes.

This book arises out of twenty-five years' experience teaching creative writing courses, most of which were centered on fiction. Over that time, it has become apparent that workshop members are increasingly less certain about basic elements of English grammar and usage and about the peculiarities that arise when the prose they are writing is creative rather than critical. This lack of knowledge results from a variety of factors, including certain less-than-inspired revisions in the English curriculum in elementary and high schools in the last decades. Perhaps even more significant is the shift away from text as we traditionally understand it toward other modes of communication and entertainment: film, television, the Internet. You could argue that this phenomenon began back in the Nineteenth Century with the invention first of the telegraph and then of the telephone. The former gave us telegraphic language (e.g., "MISSED EXPRESS STOP TAKING 5:02 STOP. . . . "); the later obviated using the written word at all.

People read texts—not merely novels or collections of verse, but also newspapers and magazines and letters—much less than they used to. The result? Aspiring writers have little experience with the conventions for something as basic as composing dialogue or punctuating a long sentence in a short story or memoir.

I put together for my students a series of handouts dealing with specific issues that seemed to be giving them trouble. I wanted to present the conventions that governed things ranging from comma usage to employing allusion. I discovered that—as with so much else in English—while certain hard-and-fast grammatical rules exist in some cases, in a great many instances what is correct is a matter of opinion. This is why we have the *MLA Style Manual and Guide to Scholarly Publishing*, *The Chicago Manual of Style*, the *Publication Manual of the American Psychological Association*, and so on—not to mention the numerous writing guides turned out annually by major publishers.

In creative work, the author confronts problems that are distinct from those dealt with by scholars or journalists. How do you best indicate an interruption in dialogue? What's the best way to transmit your characters' thoughts? When you have a foulmouthed character, how much of that foulness do you include? Even something that would seem basic—the use of serial commas to separate elements in a sequence—is not viewed consistently by editors and other writers. In addition to the volumes I just mentioned, nearly all publishers have their own rulebooks setting forth their particular "house style." While these literary styles bear considerable resemblance to one another, they can also vary considerably on particular issues.

The New Yorker's rules of usage, for example, are both notoriously detailed and notoriously eccentric. In the magazine, *martini*—the cocktail—is always capitalized and so written as *Martini*. The rationale for this is that the name comes originally from Martini & Rossi, the brand of vermouth that once played a much more important role in this mixed drink than it seems to these days.

This book approaches issues of grammar, usage, and style with a strong slant toward writers of creative prose. It is not intended to replace other manuals you may have on hand, which cover particular questions not addressed here. However, if you are writing a short story, a novel, a memoir, or some other work of creative nonfiction and a question of grammar or punctuation arises, then come here first. The result should be a manuscript which, though it may not coincide completely with the house style of an editor who reads it, will be "correct."

One great frustration for writers is that their texts don't seem to even get a reading from a publisher or agent. A major reason for this is that these manuscripts are full of problems of usage and grammar. Remember that editors are inundated with paper and with electronic text as well. They understandably look for any excuse *not* to spend fifteen minutes with a story. There is always a pile of fifty more sitting in that inbox. A submission that appears incompetently composed is one destined to be rejected.

Still, breaking conventions will be a point repeatedly stressed throughout this book. What is set forth here are conventions, and, particularly in creative work, you may wish to violate norms for any of a number of good reasons—

to create particular effects, to add emphasis, to disorient the reader. A Cormac McCarthy or an Annie Proulx does not necessarily follow the rules set forth in this book. However, these authors realize what rules they are violating and why. As you develop a personal style, you may decide when you write a particular scene that what would usually be viewed as run-on sentences are precisely what you want to employ.

That's fine, as long as you know what you are doing. Your stylistic intent always takes precedence over what is traditionally correct. Who would dare—or want—to go through *The Adventures of Huckleberry Finn* and regularize Huck's and Jim's errors in usage or insist that Faulkner break up those sonorous and obsessive outpourings of *Absalom, Absalom!* with commas, semicolons, and periods?

What you want to do is learn what the conventions of usage, punctuation, and so on are, then break them with confidence when you choose to.

Enough exhortation! What follows is divided into two parts. Part I deals with the basics of grammar, usage, and style. In Part II, we'll talk about certain larger issues that creative writers have to confront: When is obviously offensive language appropriate? What if one of your characters speaks a dialect? How much description is too much description?

Novelist William H. Gass, in his book *Tests of Time*, sets forth why all of us want to write not only movingly and powerfully but also correctly.

There is a bond between us, readers and writers, an ancient tie as old as writing is, if not as old as speech itself, a pact, a promise which the act of setting down sentences . . . implicitly solidifies . . . that what we shall say shall be as true to things and to our own hearts as we can make them, and that what we read shall be free and unforced and uttered out of what the deepest respect for the humanity language represents, whatever its contents otherwise.

Now, there's a charge for all of us.
Have at it.

PART I

The Devil in the Details: Grammar, Usage, and Stylistic Conventions

Introduction to Grammar and Usage

Like Maria in *The Sound of Music*, we're going to "start at the very begin-ning, a very good place to start." As a writer, it's incumbent upon you to know not only your ABCs and your do re mis, but also your parts of speech and what they do, your rules of punctuation and capitalization, and so on. Editors, copyreaders, or teachers of any type of writing kvetch ad nauseam about how nobody knows how to use a comma anymore, and they are largely right. "How can these people even think of being writers!" they fulminate.

This first section of the book gives you a guide to current grammatical, mechanical, and stylistic conventions of writing. Remember, however, that your best guide to all of this may not be found in these pages, which only can broadly outline how things are generally done. You should read constantly both classic and contemporary texts in order to see how authors adhere to these standards and how they violate and torque and twist them to achieve particular and distinctive effects in their work. We learn to write by reading the work of other writers. Many of the purely mechanical aspects of putting a piece of prose in print come to us by osmosis when we see how other writers set words on the page.

In this section, we'll examine basic issues as well as more complex and sophisticated ones. My assumption is that, regardless of your level of skill, you are among many sincere people who aspire to write well, and there is something touching and brave about this desire to tell the stories you have to tell. If you never acquired the basic tools to do this, that is not necessarily your fault. Still, the reality is that without these tools, your quest for a larger audience is likely to be a futile one. Many years ago, a friend remarked that ignorance is not a sin, but truculent ignorance is. If nobody ever taught you about semicolons, then you can't be blamed for using them incorrectly. If, however, you have the opportunity to learn when and how to employ them correctly but you ignore the instructions, then you don't really want somebody to read your work.

Even those who were afforded the chance to learn the conventions of grammar, usage, and style should review the building blocks of language with an eye toward identifying and discussing certain gremlins authors frequently wrestle with in producing a creative text. We'll do a quick—well, sometimes not so quick—run through the parts of speech from nouns to interjections, noting what gives us fits and how to survive these tricky rules, and then move on from there.

In our discussion of what is correct and what is not correct, remember that adherence to conventions in creative work is determined by who is speaking, who is telling your story, what story is being told, and how you as its creator have decided to tell it. Is your narrator an orphan girl who becomes the governess for a family with a mad woman in the attic in the 1840s? If so, she is going to sound a lot different than the urbane Nick Carraway in *The Great Gatsby*. If you are a Stanford graduate writing about your experience as a social worker in Idaho, the way you speak with your clients will be rendered rather differently than how you speak with former classmates. In creative prose, always aim at honesty in the presentation of the voices of those who speak in dialogue or tell your story, at the same time remaining aware that your reader must be able to follow precisely *what* is being related. You have a pact with your audience to accede to the imaginative bond of writer and reader. Your responsibility is to hook jumper cables to your imagination and that of your reader—who may be thousands of miles away and perusing your text after you've been dead for fifty years—so that she is energized and sees what you saw in your head.

Throughout this book, the admonition to be true to the voices in your work is repeated constantly.

Stop! Note this paragraph break. Note the previous sentence. Read it again!

Many constructions or expressions that are considered wrong are, nonetheless, extremely common in speech. We do not talk in Standard American English, and, in fact, it's a rare bird indeed who speaks it all the time. In a conversation between two surfers, it's entirely reasonable for one to say, "Hey, dude, Tim and me are goin' anyhow," despite the fact that the *me* should be

I, and that going ends in a *g*. Our surfer bud, in all likelihood, often drops his *g*s on participles and gerunds—those *-ing* words. If your first-person narrator is a forty-six-year-old woman with an eighth-grade education from backwoods Louisiana, she's unlikely to sound like V.S. Naipaul. A memoir of your childhood in Chicago's South Side will probably be peppered, at least in the dialogues you relate, with various so-called errors of usage—"Scope and myself saw . . . , " "Mary don't like that . . . , " and so on—as you capture the sound of the voices you recall. The fact that individuals express themselves in a way that is ungrammatical or vernacular is no reason to clean up their mistakes.

This said, it is essential that you know what the rules and conventions of grammar and usage are so that you can be conscious of your violation of them. You don't want an editor to think you are unaware of the rules for forming plurals or standard paragraphs.

Finally, I have tended in this section to take a conservative stance on numerous issues. For example, I encourage you to capitalize the names of centuries when they are employed as nouns (e.g., "In the Fourteenth Century, the plague depopulated Europe"); many publishers no longer employ this standard. Nonetheless, my traditionalism in these instances is justified. By adhering to the strictest standards, your work cannot be dismissed as incorrect.

1

Nouns and Pronouns

NOUNS
Definition and Uses

As you know, nouns name things. They can be divided into different binary categories: **proper** (*Tom, Nigeria*) and **common** (*dirt, house*), **singular** (*element, automobile*) and **plural** (*elements, automobiles*), **concrete** (*wall, mother*) and **abstract** (*courage, perfidy*). They function in the language as **subjects** and **objects** within sentences: The former (generally, at least) is the actual actor, the one who is doing something; and the latter is what is acted upon, for example, Mary [subject] slapped John [object].

Nouns can be **direct objects** and **indirect objects** of verbs. In "John hit Billy the ball," *ball* is the direct object of the verb *hit*, and *Billy* is the verb's indirect object. Nouns also serve as the objects of prepositions. In "John hit the ball to Billy," *Billy* is the object of the preposition *to*, telling us to whom the ball was hit.

Beyond these uses, nouns can function as either **subject** or **object complements**, which means they complete the definition of another noun. That noun can be the subject of a verb of being (for "Mary seems a perfect cheerleader," *Mary = cheerleader*) or the object of an active verb (in "General Wallace appointed Roland inspector plenipotentiary," *Roland = inspector plenipotentiary*). In a similar way, they also serve as **appositives**, which simply rename another noun, usually in sequence (in "Her youngest brother, Randy, drove her to work," *youngest brother = Randy*).

On the whole, we all understand how to use nouns, but a few things about them merit our attention.

Amount and Number

A common difficulty for writers is rooted in distinguishing between **number** and **amount**. It is not correct to talk about "the amount of people in the crowd" because, vast as the crowd may be, it can ultimately be counted. Even if you say, "The number of people in the crowd was so great that it could not be counted," that is, in the end, not true. What can't be counted is, for example, the enthusiasm of the crowd: "The number of people in the crowd was small, but the amount of enthusiasm was incredible." Enthusiasm is an abstraction. You can put a qualitative value on it, but not a quantitative one, at least in any precise mathematical way. Abstractions almost always demand *amount*.

A common example arises with *money.* Although we say, "Count your money," *money* is an abstraction made up concretely of coins and bills. You would never write, "She has an incredible number of money," but rather, "She has an incredible amount of money." Bills and coins can be counted, so we speak of "the number of bills in his wallet" rather than "the amount of bills."

With other nouns, the issue of what can and cannot be counted gets tricky. Despite the fact that we could theoretically establish the number of grains of rice in the Uncle Ben's box, we say "The rice is ready" rather than "The rices are ready." We treat *rice* as singular. It represents a **mass noun:** though it is finally divisible into smaller units, those units are so numerous as to approach, if not infinity, at least uncountability. An even more obvious example is *sunlight,* which we know is composed of photons but would never use with a plural verb.

Still, you can see how people can get confused.

South Dakota's wheat is the mainstay of its agricultural economy.

———

Washington's apples are the mainstay of its agricultural economy.

The plural *apples* demands a plural verb, though, arguably, Washington's fruit and South Dakota's grain are both measured not in pieces of fruit or grains of wheat but in such units as bushels or tons.

Where this whole issue is concerned, it's useful to bear in mind the difference between mass nouns and **count nouns.** You would never say "three corns," though you would say "three oranges." If you can place a numeric value before the noun (one book, eight houses), you have a count noun. If you can't (sand, rain, millet), then you have a mass noun.

This rule isn't absolute. You could obviously write "The rains come each spring" or "The sands of time keep trickling through the hourglass." The best advice, when you use *number* or *amount*, is to pause a minute to look at your expression. Most always, if you think it through, you'll make the right decision.

Collective Nouns

Things can get most problematic with certain **collective nouns**. A word such as *people* obviously refers to more than one person, but it can be dealt with as singular. The same is true for a variety of other nouns: *flock, crowd, mob, band, personnel, family,* and so on. Writers are told by grammarians that when such words refer to a group as a whole they are singular, but when they emphasize the fact that the group is composed of individuals they are plural. That's dandy, and the distinction is clear in many instances.

> Pastor William's flock is tremendously loyal.
>
> ———
>
> Pastor William's flock are constantly at each other's throats.

The first example highlights the harmony of Pastor William's congregation and its unitary devotion, while the second focuses upon its disputes and divisions. The phrase "at each other's throats" makes it extraordinarily clumsy to employ a singular verb.

Still, the whole issue can get pretty subtle. Note below how the inclusion of the article *a* shifts the sense of *people* from plural to singular.

> A people of diverse ethnicities has to learn to live together.
>
> ———
>
> People of diverse ethnicities have to learn to live together.

PRONOUNS
Definition and Uses

Pronouns are words (*I, she, you, they, who, anyone,* and so on) we substitute for nouns to help us avoid constantly repeating the same word over and over. Some pronouns are **personal** (*us, your*), while others are **relative** (*whose*) or **indefinite** (*everybody*) or **reflexive** (*themselves*). Unlike nouns in English, pronouns have "case"—their form differs according to how they are used in a sentence. Their three cases are **subjective** (or **nominative**), **objective**, and **possessive**.

The subjective personal pronouns are

I	we
you	you
he, she, it	they

In objective case, they are

me	us
you	you
him, her, it	them

The possessive pronouns are

my, mine	our, ours
your, yours	your, yours
his; her, hers; its	their, theirs

Note that the third-person singular form is the only one to distinguish gender or lack thereof—masculine, feminine, or neuter.

You can see how useful pronouns are in the following example:

Lana opened her purse and retrieved her lighter.

is a great improvement over

Lana opened Lana's purse and retrieved Lana's lighter.

The second sentence sounds absurd to us, but note the following:

Lana opened Cindy's purse and retrieved Amy's lighter.

In this sentence, substituting the pronoun *her* for any of the nouns would profoundly alter its meaning. This points up the need to be conscious of a pronoun's **antecedent**, the noun that it refers to.

Determining this can be tricky.

Knowing how upset she was about his being called up, Rob told Jim to kiss his girlfriend.

On the one hand, we presume that Rob told Jim to kiss Rob's girlfriend, but that is not clear in the sentence; the second *his* could refer to either Rob or Jim. It could be that Jim's girlfriend was deeply upset that Rob, her boyfriend's best buddy, was going on active duty.

There are instances where context might make the sense evident, but you are probably better off finding a different way to express the thought so its content is transparent. In English, this often means that you have to change the syntax of the sentence or introduce the proper name of a character to communicate your meaning.

Rob, knowing how upset his girlfriend was that he was overseas, told Jim to kiss her for him.

If the sense is different, then it could be

Knowing how upset his own girlfriend was that he was overseas, Rob told Jim to kiss his main squeeze, Stacey, for him.

Subjective and Objective Pronouns

Most writers have relatively few problems with the proper usage of **subjective** and **objective** personal pronouns, though two issues sometimes trip us up. The first of these, arguably, is no longer a problem anymore. When your character is announcing his entrance into a room, he *should* say "It is I," not "It is me." The same holds true for "It is they," "It was we," and so on. *To be*, a linking verb, should take a subject complement, not an object—that is, the pronoun following the verb should be subjective, not objective. The fact is, though, that what is correct in this case has virtually disappeared from the common parlance. Any character who says "It is I" or "It's they" sounds like either a nonnative speaker or a twit. Even in narrative rather than dialogue, a phrase like "It was we" would hit the reader's ear as peculiar. Hence, it probably makes sense to use the strictly correct form only as a means of characterization of someone in your piece who either does not know the idiomatic usage of *It is* plus an objective pronoun or is inclined to overcorrect his speech.

The other common problem (and this *is* a problem) involves the appearance of subjective pronouns (*I*, *she*, and so on) in places where objective ones (*me*, *her*) should be used. This frequently occurs in prepositional phrases with the first-person singular pronouns.

> He split it between Barbara and me.
> ─────
> She directed all her anger at Roger, Dan, and me.

not

> He split it between Barbara and I.
> ─────
> She directed all her anger at Roger, Dan, and I.

If you have trouble with this kind of construction, the easiest way to deal with it is to read the sentence to yourself as if the pronoun were the only object of the preposition. You would never have a character say

> She directed all her anger at I.

However, it sounds entirely natural to have a character say

> She directed all her anger at me.

Possessive Pronouns

Regarding **possessive pronouns**, two common errors come to mind.

The more frequent is the confusion of the possessive *its* with *it's*, the contraction of *it is*. This also occurs with *whose* and *who's*, the contraction of *who is*. The way to avoid errors is simple: Just remember that no standard possessive pronoun ever employs an apostrophe. You don't spell *hers* as *her's* or *theirs* as *their's*, and the same holds true for the pronouns *its* and *whose*. When those apostrophes show up, you have contractions, not pronouns.

Use a possessive pronoun to modify a **gerund** (a verb ending in *-ing* and used as a noun). Mistakes usually arise when the gerund is the object of a verb or preposition.

> I get so tired of his snoring (*not* "him snoring").
> ─────

Maude loves my singing (*not* "me singing").

If you use an objective pronoun (*him, me*) in such statements, then the pronoun, not the gerund (*snoring, singing*), is the object of the verb or preposition. "Maude loves me singing" indicates that she loves me when I am singing, but she may care less about me the rest of the time. *Singing* here is a present participle being used as an adjective to modify *me*, rather than as a gerund.

If what really gets to Maude is hearing me sing, then I have to use the possessive pronoun *my* to get that across.

Don't get carried away. If you observe somebody in the act of singing, it's perfectly correct to write

I saw him singing.

Whether you use a possessive pronoun or not is governed by whether that *-ing* word is a participle or a gerund, whether it is being used as an adjective or as a noun.

Number and Gender of Pronouns

Number and **gender of pronouns** can also get writers into trouble. People seem to be having a lot of problems in these areas lately, perhaps because of attempts to avoid sexism in their writing.

Words such as *anyone, each, everybody, somebody*—which are called **indefinite pronouns**—are singular and require singular pronouns when they are referred to. "Somebody put his [not *their*] feet on my chair" is correct. The same is true when you use a singular subject. For example, "A student may wish to read his [not *their*] book during the break." With *each*, simply remember the expression "To each, his own," which you certainly wouldn't render, "To each, their own." Hence, "Each person has his place within the society."

As with so much of what we're discussing, the context of the usage helps determine whether you use the form that is grammatically correct. If you use an omniscient third-person narrator, and hence follow the standard rules of English usage, then you would write "Everyone—boys and girls both—rushed to get his bicycle." However, if your character is an eighth-grade narrator named Cindy, you might very well render the same sentence "Everyone rushed to get their bicycles."

Bear in mind, however, that some indefinite pronouns are plural: *all, both, few, many, most, several, some,* and so on. These take plural verbs.

Most were unsurprised.
_____

Few understand its significance.
_____

Some retrieve their belongings.

Incidentally, such can be either singular or plural, depending on what it refers to.

Such is the destiny of a great man.
_____

Such are the destinies of great men.

The same holds true for *none.* When you intend the word to signify "not one," then it is singular ("None of the city's inhabitants was without sin."). However, if *none* obviously refers to more than one person or thing, then it takes a plural verb ("None in world history were as cruel as the legions of Rome.").

SEXISM

Some writers now employ both masculine and feminine pronouns—"Somebody put his or her feet on my chair"—though this can get awfully clumsy, especially in what you hope is a gripping narrative. The problem is that to say "Somebody put their feet" is incorrect, while "Somebody put his feet" sounds sexist. A more elegant solution is to vary the gender of your anonymous *-ones* and *-bodies*: "Anybody who wishes to take her turn now may do so" or "Anybody who thinks that he has been treated unfairly should speak up." In such instances, don't vary the pronoun in the same sentence. Too, make sure that you don't fall into precisely the kind of sexism you're trying to avoid by using the stereotypical gender for particular occupations or circumstances, for example, referring to the secretary as *she,* while the police officer is always *he.*

This is also an issue for nouns such as *student* or *reader,* which can be of either gender: "Any student who makes her decision on that basis has my support" or "Any reader who feels he is being left out should inform the teacher." However, sexism can be avoided by making that singular noun a plural one: "Any students who make their decisions on that basis have my support." This neatly solves the whole problem because *their* with the plural noun is correct.

Still, in creative work, it is easiest to stick to the convention of the masculine pronoun as the general pronoun, even though that may strike you as sexist. Even varying the pronouns in your narrative (much less insisting on *him or her* or *his or hers*) clots up the prose and draws attention to your politically correct earnestness. Down the road, the use of *their* with a singular antecedent may become standard, just as we noted that the expression "It's me" has, for all practical purposes, become "correct" English. We might even fall back on the neuter pronoun *it* and its variants much more frequently ("Each student may chose its own seat").

Everyone may not agree with this, and there is a real question as to whether writers should buy into this convention. For the present, we're stuck with rules that were made in the days of high patriarchy. It is up to you to decide if this issue is of sufficient significance to you to attempt alteration of what remains common usage, though you should remember that this is more a political than an aesthetic choice. To take a progressive stand is fine, but don't complain when your commitment makes your submission to certain presses an exercise in postage. Change costs and always has, and the International Octopus Communications Group may shy away from you. At the end of the day, you have to make a choice as to just how far you are willing to compromise certain principles in order to get published.

I do not mean this lightly.

In a science fiction story you could regularize throughout *s/he* in narrative, but, even in that very forgiving and laid-back genre, it's a gamble. Your motivation may be admirable, but, unless you deal with a press that is dedicated to the same ideals as yours or you are a well-established writer, you may find that editors are simply annoyed by your insistence on avoiding the language's ingrained sexism.

That's not a happy thing to say, but that's the way it is.

ONE VS. YOU

One (the "loneliest number," according to a long-ago rock song) is a third-person singular pronoun, and it takes a third-person singular verb. In fiction, *one* shows up rarely, or at least it should. It is frankly fussy sounding. It's often used in essays and the like to avoid the more informal and personal *you*: "One often reads in the newspaper that politicians are corrupt" vs. "You often read in the newspaper that politicians are corrupt." God forbid, that in a serious piece of political commentary or psychological exegesis, we should actually be informal and personal!

In any case, do not use these two pronouns—*you* and *one*—interchangeably in the same sentence, as in "One may wish that you had gone into town." Write either "One may wish that one had gone into town" or "One may wish that he had gone into town" or "You may wish that you had gone into town." As you can see, the first two examples are a bit on the stiff side. It's certainly possible for you to have a character or narrator who would employ this rather formal diction or for you to want to strike a particularly formal tone in the narrative itself:

> In those days, when one looked out over London, it still possessed an odd coziness in comparison to what it seems today.

That phrasing, though, has an undeniably arch or archaic feel to it. If that isn't your intent, stick with

> In those days, when you looked out over London, it had an odd coziness in comparison to how it feels today.

The use of *you* depends a lot on the tone of the narrative being created, in that we use this pronoun frequently in informal speech as being synonymous with *everyone*. With a confiding first- or even third-person narrator—one who makes us feel we are literally being told a story—then the use of *you* is entirely logical: "You've met Tom's kind of guy before. . . . " Your use of this pronoun will be determined in large part by the voice that you employ in the narrative you present.

Relative Pronouns

That, what, and **which** are sometimes pronouns and sometimes adjectives: "That settles it," "You decided to do what!" and "Which is which?" demonstrate their use as pronouns. In "I want that one," "What answer did you give her?" and "Which shoes did you buy?" they function as adjectives.

When used as pronouns, these words are called **relative pronouns**. The other members of this little tribe are *who, whoever, whom, whomever,* and *whose.* The first four of these give people fits.

Things look pretty straightforward on the surface: *Who* and *whoever* are subjective pronouns.

Who would have thought it?
___

Whoever would do something like that should be shot!

Whom and *whomever* are objective.

The car was sold to whom?
___

I will take bids for the car from whomever.

Things get sticky because these words are often part of longer clauses that themselves function as subjects or objects. In the foregoing examples, the clause "Whoever would do something like that" is the subject of the sentence. In a sentence such as the following, the tendency is to overcorrect and use *whomever* rather than *whoever.*

I will take bids for the car from whoever cares to make one.

Whoever is correct here because the object of the preposition *from* is the entire clause "whoever cares to make one," not just the pronoun. The pronoun *whoever* functions as the subject in this clause, so the subjective case is properly employed.

Some grammarians suggest a nice little trick to avoid getting befuddled by this entire business: If you can't decide whether to use *who* or *whom,* substitute or insert a personal pronoun at the point they appear.

The car was sold to *them?* [The pronoun is objective.]
___

They would have thought it? [*They* is a subjective pronoun.]

As you can see, you're far less likely to be confused using this simple aid. Can you imagine that "them" would have thought it?

Reflexive Pronouns

For one class of pronouns we haven't touched on a few words might be useful. These are the **reflexive pronouns**, those that end in *-self* or *-selves*: *myself, herself, ourselves,* and so on. These pronouns reflect back on previous nouns or pronouns and intensify them.

> Doris herself turned out to be the culprit.
>
> ――――
>
> Marco insisted on doing it himself.

It is unsurprisingly incorrect to employ a reflexive pronoun in an instance where there is nothing to reflect. Nonetheless, it's common to see reflexive pronouns replacing subjective or objective ones in dialogue to indicate colloquial speech: "Alice and myself were the only two not invited." In standard English, that sentence should begin with "Alice and I." Again, depending on which character is speaking or narrating, you could employ the incorrect form with no problem.

Agreement

Finally, keep an eye out in your sentences to be sure that your verbs, nouns, and pronouns are all in proper agreement. Recently, I found in a *Time* magazine from 1999 the following sentence in reference to two different groups supporting the presidential candidacy of George W. Bush:

> Both have placed their hopes in the son, and last week they were left shaking their head.

Read the sentence carefully, then think about the image it evokes. Everything is clicking along merrily in the plural until we hit the last word in the sentence. Suddenly, "both" camps are shaking "their head." Two groups with but one head? We won't even discuss the politics this implies.

Obviously, the sentence should conclude with *heads*, not *head,* but the error presumably passed from writer to editor to copyeditor to typesetter—professionals all—with no one picking up on it.

If this can happen to *Time,* it can happen to you.

2

Verbs

DEFINITION AND CATEGORIES

A **verb** is the engine of a sentence. Strictly speaking, without a verb, there *is* no sentence but merely a fragment, while a verb standing alone ("Halt!" "Repeat!") can be a sentence in itself. Verbs express either **action** ("Amy skipped," "Ronnie considered") or a **state of being** ("He is," "Walter seems"). They can be **transitive** or **intransitive**: The former type takes an object ("Sandra drinks water"); the latter does not ("Lorraine runs very fast").

In English, verbs have **number, person, voice, tense,** and **mood.** A verb's number is singular or plural, while its person is first (used with *I, we*), second (used with *you, you* [all]), or third (used with *he, she, it, they*). Note that only in third person the verb is different in the singular and the plural: "She thinks," but "They think." To contrast first person, for example, "I think," and "We think."

In terms of voice, **active verbs** are used for subjects that do something ("Milly plays the piano"), and **passive verbs** are used with subjects that are acted upon ("The piano is played by Milly").

Tense indicates the time that the action or state of being referred to by the verb took place or existed. Of the six tenses in English, three are **simple**—past, present, and future—and three are **perfect**—present perfect, past perfect, and future perfect. For example:

She dances [present].

———

She danced [past].

———

She will dance [future].

———

She has danced [present perfect].

―――

She had danced [past perfect].

―――

She will have danced [future perfect].

There is a subset of tense referred to as **form**, which linguists call **aspect**. This appears in **progressive** verbs. These follow the pattern present, past, and future and indicate ongoing action.

She is dancing.

―――

She was dancing.

―――

She will be dancing.

―――

She has been dancing.

―――

She had been dancing.

―――

She will have been dancing.

Mood, which we'll discuss at some length a little later, marks whether a verb expresses a fact, a command, a wish, or a possibility. English has three moods: **indicative** (employed in statements of fact and in most questions), **imperative** (used in commands and requests), and **subjunctive**. The first and second moods are pretty easy. Most of the time, we employ the indicative mood.

We hurried to make the train.

―――

"Who spoke first?"

The imperative only arises with regard to the second-person form of a verb, singular or plural, and is usually—though not always—signaled by the repression of the subject *you*.

"Hurry!"

———

"Speak up, please."

———

"You go, girl!"

The subjunctive we'll get to in "More on Moods" on page 29.

Auxiliary Verbs

To create certain tenses or forms of a verb, we employ **auxiliary** or **helping** verbs. These are, in fact, verbs in their own right, and they have their own meanings and can stand alone. The principal ones are *to be* (used in progressive forms, e.g., "I was thinking about it"), *to have* (used in the perfect tenses, e.g., "I will have written three papers by Friday"), and another verb we haven't yet mentioned, *to do*, which appears most frequently in questions and negative commands.

"Did he really tell you that?"

———

"Don't you dare!"

Still, *to do* can also show up as an intensifier of the main verb.

"You did complete all your work."

———

"He does understand what you mean."

To do also represents the sole example in English of what is called a **pro-verb** (not to be confused with a proverb). As you might expect, a pro-verb functions in the way a pronoun does; that is, it takes the place of a verb. Like pronouns, pro-verbs must have an antecedent so that we know what action (as opposed to person or thing) is being referred to. Here are a couple of examples of *to do* in its function as a pro-verb.

She had no time to bake, but I did.

———

"Who broke the vase? Did you?"

PROBLEMS WITH TENSE

Many writers seem to have trouble maintaining consistent **tense**. Conventionally, stories are written in the past tense, with the past perfect ("had run," for example) indicating something that occurred before the time in which the story is set. In the following, I have italicized the verbs so you can see what I mean.

> Larry *was* a guy who never quite *fathomed* who he *was* and what he *wanted* from life. From one year to the next, his personality *changed* entirely. In the eighth grade, he *had been* such an angel that what few friends he *had* then *called* him "teacher's pet" and worse. So when he *entered* high school after a family vacation to Laguna Beach, California, nobody *was* quite *prepared* for his leather jeans, his nose ring, the brass knuckles in his pocket, or the "go ahead, make my day" sneer on his face.

When the eighth grade is referred to, the past perfect tense is used to mark this as belonging to a farther past ("had been such an angel"). It's usually only necessary to do this *once*, as you can see in the conclusion of that sentence, which continues in the simple past ("friends he had" rather than "friends he had had").

That single helping verb signals to the reader that you are talking about something that occurred in a past prior to the time of the story. If you continue the piece, do so in the simple past:

> . . . In the eighth grade, he had been such an angel that what few friends he had then called him "teacher's pet" and worse. So, when he entered high school after a family vacation to Laguna Beach, California, nobody was quite prepared for his leather jeans, his nose ring, the brass knuckles in his pocket, or the "go ahead, make my day" sneer on his face.
>
> Larry? we thought. Larry: well behaved, well adjusted, just, well, a totally well kind of guy. And now he was some kind of coastal mutant that most of us kids in Greenville had only seen on the Internet.

You can see how smoothly this reads—how we can distinguish between the good-boy Larry that everybody was accustomed to in junior high school and the teenage-mutant-ninja Larry that came back from Laguna Beach.

Of course, it is possible to write a story in the present tense ("Larry is a boy who has never quite figured out . . . "), and many authors have done so over the years. The attraction of this technique is that the present makes a story more intense and immediate, though that idea is clearly arguable. Present tense is conventional in the narrative interpolations in screenplays and dramatic scripts ("Randall moves to the door and opens it"), as well as in critical work when action from a text under study is related.

> As Hamlet watches Claudius watching the players perform their dumb show, he provides a running commentary, identifying each character. Notably, he identifies the murderer of the sleeping king not as his "brother" but as his "nephew."

Why these conventions differ is anybody's guess. In everyday life we employ both forms in oral narratives, for example: "So I got to work and Mary said to me . . . " and "So I get to work and Mary says to me. . . . " Too, many writers have shifted between past and present tense as of means of distinguishing between narration and a character's thoughts, between reality and a dream, and so on.

If you can come up with a compelling reason to narrate your story in present tense (e.g., your narrator dies at the end—ho hum!), then do it. Most of the time, make it easy on yourself and stick with the past tense.

Temporally Unlimited Description

Apprentice writers sometimes get confused when narrating in the past tense and deciding how best to put forth information (about characters, situations, and places) that is **temporally unlimited**, or continuingly true. Note that the earlier example began with the statement "Larry was a guy" despite the fact that Larry—barring serious psychological circumstances that would eventually necessitate gender reassignment—was always a guy, is presently a guy, and will remain a guy for the rest of his natural life.

Some languages have distinct past tenses: one for those things that are initiated and completed in the past; and another for denoting gender, occupation, eye color, and other long-term or immutable characteristics, as well as for things that are recurrent, take place over an extended period of past time, or were in progress when another event occurred. In Spanish, for example, by using one past tense or the other, you could distinguish between those things about Larry that were ongoing characteristics ("Larry was a guy") and those things that were over and done with ("he entered high school").

For good or ill, we have this capacity only in a very limited way in English thanks to the past progressive tense. In English, we say, "You were eating when he arrived." The first phrase is in the past progressive form—the conjugated verb *to be* plus the present participle *eating*—while the second is in past tense.

To bring this digression to a close, when you're narrating in the past, you should generally *stay in the past.* Even though something may *continue* to be true about a character or situation ("Marilyn was a nurse," "My mom always said so," "Chicago faced the lake"), *don't* switch to the present tense. All that does is confuse the reader, and it often confuses the author as well.

Tense in Dialogue Mixed With Narrative Passages

One other place apprentice writers frequently get into trouble is in **dialogue passages.** Characters use the present tense when they speak, while the narration itself is in past tense.

> Sarah turned around. "I'm going to the store, Jamie. Do you want to come?" she asked.
> "No, I don't think so," he replied.

The dialogue here uses present tense ("I am going." "Do you want?"), but the action took place in the past ("turned," "asked," "replied"). A writer who does not pay attention tends to continue the narrative in the same tense as that in the dialogue. The result is sloppy passages such as the following:

> Marcy rounded the corner and found herself face-to-face with Walter.
> "I'm looking for you! I cannot believe you're saying the things you're saying about Mike and me! Are you crazy?"
> Walter is shocked. He takes a step back and looks confused.

The author shifted to Marcy's speech, which is in present tense, then incorrectly continued in the present tense in the narrative, which to this point had been in past tense. This is, most often, a consequence of either haste or insufficient editing.

Modal Verbs

When you narrate in the past tense, be careful with what used to be called **conditional verbs** and are now referred to as verbs that include **modal auxiliaries**: *can, could, may, might, must, ought, would, should,* and sometimes *shall* and *will.* These auxiliaries allow us to offer advice or to express capability, determination, probability, wishes, and requests.

Remember, *don't* employ the present tense verb *can* but rather its past tense form, *could,* when your narrative is in the past tense. In similar instances, use the conditional *would* instead of the future tense *will.* Remember that the past tense of *may* is *might.*

However, *might* is also a modal auxiliary in its own right. It is similar in its sense to *may* but implies a greater degree of doubt or unlikelihood. This is subtle, but most native speakers can distinguish this nuance.

I may go to London in the spring.

_____

I might go to London in the spring.

Since the past tense of *might* is also *might,* just as it is of *may,* the distinction between these two auxiliaries can't be made by the past tense form alone; it must be indicated by context.

Note the differences below in the quoted vs. the narrated renditions of what Tara said to Lisa.

"I don't know," Tara said to Lisa. "I may go back to Marvin or I may not."

_____

"I don't know," Tara said to Lisa, "I might go back to Marvin or I might not."

_____

Tara told Lisa that she might go back to Marvin or she might not.

_____

Tara said, "I will get back together with Marvin if I can."

——

Tara told Lisa she would get back together with Marvin if she could.

Finally, a common literary tic of apprentice writers is the overuse of *would*. It constitutes a strange kind of stutter, as if it has to be emphasized to the reader that something is a repeated condition. Consider these examples:

We would go to the store regularly.

——

We would have dinner every night on TV tables.

For these sentences, the past tense is perfectly adequate:

We went to the store regularly.

——

We had dinner every night on TV tables.

Modal auxiliaries can be useful in your work, but don't depend on them. When you can stick with the simple tenses, do so.

ACTIVE AND PASSIVE VOICE

As long as we're discussing verbs, we might as well mention the old saw about favoring active verbs over passive ones. Compare these sentences, variations using first active and then passive voice:

Olaf hit the ball.

versus

The ball was hit by Olaf.

——

On the following Friday, they stormed the citadel.

versus

The citadel was stormed by them the following Friday.

A college friend of mine once told me about an exercise his class undertook in a Catholic school. The brother had each student write an in-class essay;

then he told the students to count the number of passive verbs and deduct that number from one hundred to get their scores on the essay. His theory ran that we think of passive verbs as sounding more elegant, more objective, and somehow more sophisticated than active verbs, and hence we overuse them.

There's absolutely nothing wrong with the passive voice, and its use is sometimes almost unavoidable. In some instances, perhaps, you may justifiably favor it. Passive voice takes the emphasis away from the executor of the action. For example, "Jane was killed by a train" emphasizes poor Jane rather than the train that killed her; the train gets the emphasis in "A train killed Jane." Still, active verbs almost always have greater impact on a reader.

Especially in creative writing, keep an eye out for passive voice. If it seems to show up a lot, ask yourself why you're depending on it, and see if you can recast the sentences and employ active verbs. Most of the time, you *can* do it, and the sentences will be smoother and more powerful if you do.

MORE ON MOODS

Other languages have subjunctive tenses. In English, we just have our moods.

Recall that we have three different moods in English: indicative, imperative, and subjunctive. This last one gives us trouble, so we're conscious of it; the others come so naturally, we don't even think about them.

The indicative mood, which we use most frequently, is simple declaration. We merely indicate something or state a fact or observation.

Bob is a complete idiot.

———

Larry's reaction represented the mindless and robotic response we had come to anticipate from a man in way over his head.

Most questions are composed in the indicative mood.

"What is the point of continuing this?"

———

"Do you know where Laura went?"

The imperative mood, meanwhile, is employed in instances of urgency or command and is often indicated by syntactical peculiarities. Frequently, this is the complete absence of a subject.

"Do it!"
———

"Run!"
———

"Help!"
———

"Don't you back talk me!"

The subject of all of these is *you*, though in all but the last it is understood, not present.

The subjunctive, our tricky mood in English, is employed primarily for statements and questions expressing things impossible or contrary to fact. Subjunctive mood usually involves the use of *were* instead of the anticipated form of the verb *to be*. Its use is often signaled by verbs such as *wish* or *hope* or by such conjunctions as *if*, *as if*, or *as though*.

Are you confused yet? It really is pretty simple. Read the following examples:

I wish I were king.
———

She treated me as if I were Raul.
———

As though Pat were a bird, he flew over our heads.
———

Wouldn't it be nice if Lee could come?
———

The general imagined that, if only he were twenty years younger, he might have won the battle.

To run down the list: I'm not king, so this is contrary to fact. Likewise, I'm not Raul, nor is Pat a bird. It looks like Lee's not going to show up. It's impossible for the general to be twenty years younger than he presently is or to win a battle that he has already lost.

We do have instances in English where we employ something similar to the **present subjunctive** tense that exists in other languages. You have come upon this, even if you're not aware of it. You encounter phrases, often commonplaces, in which the subject seems to demand a verb other than the one that appears. This is because the subjunctive form is often used to express hope, requirement, or demand.

Long live the King!

———

God save us.

———

Protocol demanded the senior ambassador take his place at the head of the table.

If these sentences were simply declarations of fact, they would use indicative forms of the verb.

The King lives long.

———

God saves us.

———

The senior ambassador took his place at the head of the table.

Note that in some subjunctive phrases, often introduced with *if,* the ordinary forms of the verb *to be* (e.g., *is, are*) are replaced by *be.*

We'll invite her if need be.

———

If there be danger, she can be counted on.

This can get more complex, in that the subjunctive comes into play when conditional situations or instances of concession, requirement, suggestion, supposition, expectation, or recommendation are evoked. This is obvious only in the third-person singular, where, rather than the anticipated form of the verb ending in *s,* you use what amounts to the third-person plural form (with no *s*).

I advise he think it over more carefully.

———

We insist Lonnie score well on the test.

Don't get overenthusiastic with the subjunctive. Consider this sentence, which is similar to a previous example.

I dreamed I was king.

Although my kingship is contrary to literal fact, it is consistent with fact in that context of the dream.
The same holds true when you are talking about an error of perception.

Olga thought that I was Raul.

Though I am not Raul, Olga thought otherwise, even though she was mistaken.

PHRASAL VERBS

A wonderful phenomenon in English, the **phrasal verb**, is worth mentioning here. A phrasal verb is formed by adding one or two or three words to a root verb. These other words are referred to as "particles," so sometimes this kind of verb is called a **particle verb**. The particles themselves tend to be drawn from the ranks of prepositions (*with*, *in*) or adverbs (*away*, *out*). The meaning of a phrasal verb changes depending which particle is added. For example:

screw around
_____

screw over
_____

screw up

All of these have different meanings: "to do nothing in particular," "to treat unfairly," "to make a mistake." None of these relate much to the meaning, either literal or colloquial, of the verb *screw*, though, if you analyze them metaphorically, you can see what their origins likely were. Phrasal verbs represent a type of **idiomatic expressions**, and they are something you just have to learn, which most of us do without even thinking about it.

The tricky thing about phrasal verbs is how they handle objects. With some, the object can either fall after the entire phrasal verb or separate its elements.

Tommy really screwed up the experiment.

Tommy really screwed the experiment up.

However, you would employ only the first in the following.

I ran across the book yesterday.

not

I ran the book across yesterday.

If the direct object of the phrasal verb is a pronoun, it usually has to fall between the two elements of the verb.

Tommy really screwed it up.

not

Tommy really screwed up it.

You can see an exception, however, in the other example, in which the pronoun has to follow the entire verb phrase for the sentence to make sense.

I ran across it yesterday.

not

I ran it across yesterday.

Overuse of Phrasal Verbs

Be cautious about overusing phrasal verbs when simple verbs do the job more efficiently. Have a look at the following sentences:

Paul climbed up the fire escape to the roof. **Better:** Paul climbed the fire escape to the roof.

Matilda sat down on the chair. **Better:** Matilda sat on the chair.

Larry ate up all the fruitcake. **Better**: Larry ate all the fruitcake.

Climbing to the roof is an action of going up. Sitting is normally a downward motion, which is why we say "sit up" when someone is slouching or lying down. If Larry ate all the fruitcake, then he ate it all, period.

You can argue that employing the phrasal verb is a means of intensifying the expression, and that justification works in certain instances. However, make sure that this is the effect you're aiming at before you substitute the verb plus a particle for the simple verb alone.

VERBALS (PARTICIPLES, GERUNDS, AND INFINITIVES)

To bring this disquisition on one part of speech to a close, we should address what some grammarians refer to as a **verbal**, a form of a verb which functions as a different part of speech in a sentence.

The first of these is the **participle**, either present or past, which you're familiar with from the progressive and perfect forms of verbs.

She was swimming when I arrived.

——

I had telephoned him just before the accident.

These -*ing* and -*ed* forms, however, can also appear in sentences as adjectives. Remember that past participles are sometimes irregular, and can end in -*en*, -*n*, -*t*, and so on, as *forgotten, spoken, bent*.

He always found swimming girls remarkably sexy.

——

Telephoned responses are simply not acceptable.

——

The forgotten treasures remained in the attic.

If the present participle (-*ing*) is employed as noun, we call it a **gerund**.

Swimming represents an excellent way to stay fit.

The third kind of verbal is the **infinitive**, the basic form of the verb consisting of *to* plus the verb in question, such as *to sigh, to elevate, to remind,* and so on. Infinitives appear in sentences as nouns, adjectives, and adverbs. The following examples demonstrate **present infinitives**.

> To swim was his greatest dream.
> ___
>
> The book was difficult to read.
> ___
>
> Peter was the first to arrive.

One issue that always arises in connection with this verbal is the **split infinitive**. Some insist that it is never correct to insert an adverb between the *to* and the verb of the infinitive. Far too much is made of this issue, which, in the end, is one of style, not grammar. Nine times out of ten, there is no particular reason to split the elements of an infinitive. Doing this is sometimes useful, though, because interpolating the adverb tends to emphasize it.

> I'd advise you to consider your options fully.
> ___
>
> I'd advise you to fully consider your options.

or

> She had never thought to pursue it seriously.
> ___
>
> She had never thought to seriously pursue it.

In the first pair, splitting the infinitive throws stress onto *fully*. In the second example, you can see the same phenomenon. Indeed, in that instance, splitting the infinitive clarifies the fact that *seriously* modifies *to pursue* rather than the main verb, *had thought*.

Another kind of infinitive is the **perfect infinitive**. This isn't a tough one, folks. It is simply the perfect tense employing the infinitive.

> She planned to have finished the course before autumn.
> ___
>
> After that, Mike seemed to have lost all his spunk.
> ___

The team was crushed to have seen such a bungle.

This construction can be a little clumsy, but it's perfectly grammatical. Writers tend to have problems with perfect infinitives, employing them when the main verb of the sentence is already a perfect verb. In that case, a present infinitive is sufficient. This is a kind of overcorrection resulting from a needless attempt to keep all of the verbs in a single tense. Hence, rather than

Edgar had hoped to have resumed his studies immediately.

you simply write

Edgar had hoped to resume his studies immediately.

The verbs in creative pieces are probably the most important words of all. They are the Martina Navratilovas, the Elvis Stojkos, the Sammy Sosas of your work. They provide the muscle to drive your text forward. Don't get too inventive, but do include that unanticipated verb that can suddenly set a sentence soaring. Apprentice writers too often concentrate on modifiers of one kind or another to lend power to their prose, but the verbs most often kick the reader in the head—or wherever else!—and make him pay attention to the text.

3

Modifiers

DEFINITION

Theoretically, a language could be composed of nothing more than nouns and verbs. Most conversations, however, would probably get real dull real fast. Indications are that it did not take humankind long to realize that they wanted to express the kind of color, nuance, and richness that only **modifiers** can provide.

Words we think of primarily as nouns sometimes fulfill this function ("*mother* love," "*Xerox* copies"), as do past and present participles and infinitives ("*dreaded* moment," "*interesting* subject," "*to-do* list"). Pure modifiers are **adjectives** and **adverbs**. Adjectives describe nouns; adverbs modify verbs, adjectives, and other adverbs. Where nouns, verbals, phrases, and clauses that modify are concerned, their function within a sentence is defined as either **adjectival** or **adverbial**.

Adjectives and adverbs are docile beasts. They are relatively changeless and cause no worry about mood or case or conjugations, though they do alter in form when employed in comparison. With phrases and clauses, things get slightly dicier. On the whole, writers are comfortable with modifiers.

TWO COMMON PROBLEMS: OVERWRITING AND ABSTRACTION

The ease of working with modifiers may actually be the biggest problem that arises in creative work. The malignant proliferation of modifiers is probably the most common kind of **overwriting**. Apprentice writers, drunk with the language's multitudinous and previously un-thought-of possibilities, tumble ecstatically into a wild intoxication in which mobs of modifiers stagger and

reel wildly through sonorous sentences, leaving the poor reader straining—
nay, truly stupefied!—before the armada of adjectives, the army of adverbs, the
phalanxes of phrases, and columns of clauses marching without cease through
paragraph after endless paragraph like marauding barbarians through con-
quered and abject Rome.

As you can see, this temptation does not afflict only beginners.

The goal in your writing is to be exact and colorful without clotting up
your expression with needless or repetitive words. In the overinflated sentence
above, you can see how, individually, the various modifiers—adjectives, adverbs, phrases, and clauses—are fine. But their cumulative effect is overwhelm-
ing and unintentionally comic. When you reread something you have written,
take note as to whether every noun has its adjective, every verb has its adverb,
and so on. If so, you're trying too hard or choosing nouns and verbs that are
not as specific and striking as they should be.

An opposite but equally significant problem can arise when modifiers are
too few or too **abstract** or uninteresting. Simply telling your reader that "Carrie was beautiful" doesn't say much. How was she beautiful? In that busty and
full-figured way of the forties and fifties, like the look of Jane Russell or
Marilyn Monroe? Like the icons of the latter part of the Twentieth Century:
slim and even slightly androgynous? Is Carrie's a classic or an exotic beauty?
Is her beauty physical or spiritual? What specifically do you want your audience
to envision?

The solution to this problem is not a "wanted poster" description: "Carrie
was five foot two, weighed one hundred and two pounds, had brown hair and
green eyes, a good figure, and pretty legs." The inadequacy of such a passage
is threefold. First, for someone not trained in law enforcement, precise heights
and weights are largely pointless. Can you really visualize the difference between a woman who is five-two and one who is five-four? One who weighs
one hundred ten pounds vs. one who weighs ninety-eight pounds? Second,
vague modifiers clutter, not enhance, a description. What constitutes a "good"
figure or "pretty" legs? Beyond these issues, all this description is delivered in
one fell swoop, which neither produces the impact of a description more fully
integrated into the text nor reflects how we perceive people when we meet
them in real life.

Revealing characteristics of a person—both the physical self and the
personality—more gradually is a useful, effective technique. Additionally,

give the readers a sense of what a character looks like via details that tell something distinctive and easily perceptible about the character.

Rob had always found Carrie beautiful, from the very first time they met. Initially, it was those sea green eyes, somehow astonishing against her complexion the color of caffe latte. That, and the way she moved. She had the supple grace of a cat—not a house cat, but something like a cheetah, some swift and long-limbed wild thing that demanded both admiration and respect.

You can see here how the author gives some very specific details but allows us readers to construct Carrie on our own. We don't know how much Carrie weighs, how tall she is, or what her breasts or her behind is like. We know that Rob finds her attractive, but one of the wonderful things about prose as opposed to film is that it is up to the readers to "make" a character, and my vision of what Carrie looks like may be very different from yours. However, if this story gets made into a movie starring Halle Berry, that's who we both will see when we think of Carrie. Prose involves a kind of collusion between you and your reader that the visual media can never imitate.

COMPARATIVE AND SUPERLATIVE DEGREES

To get to more concrete issues, let's first turn to the adjectives and adverbs used when two or more things are compared. Beyond the simple form of the modifier (*dark*, *fully*), these words have two degrees: **comparative** and **superlative**. The first is employed when *two* things, people, places, and so on are compared; the second, when more than two are compared.

Tuesday night seemed darker than Monday night [comparative].

Tuesday night was the darkest he had ever experienced [superlative].

In Natasha's presentation, Plato's position was more fully explained than Aristotle's [comparative].

In Natasha's presentation, the vision of the stoics was the most fully explained of all those of the Greek philosophical schools [superlative].

Adverb forms generally do not change when used for comparison. The root word remains the same, and its degree is indicated by a preceding adverb (e.g., *more, best, least, worst*).

Adjectives are a little more complicated. One-syllable words generally become comparative and superlative forms by taking on the suffixes *-er* and *-est*: *madder, maddest; whiter, whitest; truer, truest.* Exceptions to this include irregular words such as *good* (*better, best*) and *bad* (*worse, worst*).

To illustrate another exception, the degrees of *pleased* are not *pleaseder* and *pleasedest*; they are *more pleased* and *most pleased.* This is so despite the fact we would usually write *tireder* and *tiredest.* Determining which way to go on this is sometimes tricky and depends on convention, sound, and meaning. With *true*, we may say: "A truer word was never spoken." However, in some contexts we might—for emphasis—opt for *more true:* "How you could believe her version of the story was more true than my own is beyond me!"

With two-syllable adjectives, the same variation in making degree forms occurs. Some take suffixes (*silly, silliest*); some take an adverb (*thoughtful, more thoughtful*). Words ending in *y* usually take *-er* and *-est*: *prettiest, goofier, shadiest.*

For root words of more than two syllables, the convention is to use adverbs to indicate degree: *more affable, most wonderful, least scandalous*, and so on.

Take note that there is some controversy about whether certain adjectives (*perfect* and *unique* are the most common examples) can actually have degree. The notion is that perfection and uniqueness are absolute; that is, if something is "less perfect," then it wasn't perfect to begin with. Some take this position with regard to, for example, shapes: *cylindrical, round, square.* If something is "rounder" than something else, is that other something else round at all? Despite all this, people have been finding the taste of one wine to be "more unique" than that of another, and so on. Whether you view these kinds of words as absolute is largely up to you.

Retaining the distinction between comparative and superlative in the language is extremely useful, and it is an area where novice writers often fall down. When we read "Doris was the elder of the sisters" and "Monique was the eldest of the sisters," we automatically know (or should!) that Doris has one sister and Monique has more than one. People can get lazy about these kinds of distinctions in their discourse, but writers should not.

DANGLING AND MISPLACED MODIFIERS

Many languages have means of indicating that a particular word modifies another even if the words are widely separated in the sentence. In English, this isn't the case. We depend heavily upon **syntax**—the order of the words—to determine a sentence's meaning. As a general rule, a modifier should fall as close as possible to the word that it modifies.

The most common problem that arises with modifiers is bad placement in a sentence, rendering them either **dangling** or **misplaced**.

Dangling Modifiers

A dangling modifier is easy to spot, is usually the product of haste, and most often falls at the opening of a sentence. A dangling modifier has no logical referent, so the reader can't figure out what the word is supposed to describe.

Nearing the hospital, the explosion took me by surprise.

What does "nearing the hospital" refer to? It would appear to modify *explosion*, but it obviously can't. The writer intends the referent to be the speaker—*me*, or rather an *I* that simply isn't in the sentence. Instead, that poor phrase just dangles out there, twisting slowly, slowly in the wind.

Shifting the phrase elsewhere in the sentence clarifies things, though both of the following alternatives come out a bit clunky:

The explosion took me, nearing the hospital, by surprise.

——

The explosion took me by surprise nearing the hospital.

The best bet is to rewrite the sentence so that the sense of the modifier is apparent and the entire thought reads smoothly.

As I neared the hospital, the explosion took me by surprise.

——

The explosion took me by surprise as I was nearing the hospital.
Or perhaps best of all:
Nearing the hospital, I was surprised by the explosion.

Misplaced Modifiers

A misplaced modifier represents a somewhat more sophisticated type of error in that the referent is ambiguous rather than missing. The reader can't determine— or determines contrary to the author's intent—what word the adjective, adverb, phrase, or clause is related to. As noted, the placement of a modifier within a sentence has a significant role in defining its meaning, and writers most often falter with phrases or clauses. Still, even individual words can end up misplaced, and this occurs most frequently with **limiting modifiers** such as *almost, hardly, not, only,* and *the like,* as illustrated in the following:

By the time Lucia arrived, all the guests were not drunk.

What this says is that when Lucia got to the party, everybody was sober. If that's the intended meaning, the sentence is phrased correctly. If, however, the meaning of the sentence is that, when Lucia arrived, some guests were drunk and some weren't, then the modifier *not* is misplaced. For the sense to be clear, instead of falling before *drunk, not* should fall before *all.*

By the time Lucia arrived, not all the guests were drunk.

Authors get confused by this because speech has ways of cuing the listener to the meaning of a sentence. These do not exist when the same words are written down. If our example were spoken, the speaker might put emphasis on particular words and alter the apparent syntactical sense of the sentence.

"By the time Lucia arrived, *all* of the guests were *not* drunk!"

This provides the sense that not all of the guests were drunk. However, to make that clear in print, you have to fall back on underlining or italics or some other visual variant, which can be distracting, or worse, make your work look amateurish.

Misplacement is more common with phrases and clauses. When we know what we intend to say or we think the referent is evident, we can get careless. This can result in some real howlers.

Shocked, she read the note about Carla's suicide tacked to the bulletin board.

The way the sentence is structured, it can be read to mean that the desperate but apparently ingenious Carla somehow managed to crucify herself on the bulletin board in a gruesome contemporary variant of the death of a thousand cuts. One can only imagine the number of tiny tack wounds she absorbed before the poor dear gave up the ghost.

Unless this is a scene from a dark comedy or the fourteenth sequel to some teen slasher film, the prepositional phrase and the verb clause in the sentence have to be reversed:

> Shocked, she read the note, tacked to the bulletin board, about Carla's suicide.

In English, you always have to be concerned about sequence, about how words, phrases, and clauses connect with one another. This may be a drag, but it is the way our language works. Make sure, especially in your longer sentences, that all the elements link up logically.

UNNECESSARY PHRASAL MODIFIERS

One thing I've noted in apprentice writing is the substitution of a prepositional phrase where either an adjective or an adverb would be more effective. Particularly if overused, such phrases lead to clumsiness and wordiness in a piece of prose. To give you a notion of what I mean, take a look at these examples.

> She walked to the door of the bedroom.
> ——
> Marvis studied the painting in awe.
> ——
> Hans picked up the mess without thought.
> ——
> In haste, she ducked into the closet.

These can be more effectively put over by substituting simple words for the prepositional phrases.

> She walked to the bedroom door.
> ——

Awed, Marvis studied the painting.

——

Hans, unthinking, picked up the mess.

——

She hastily ducked into the closet.

I'm not sure why people shy away from adjectives in these contexts. This avoidance of adverbs may arise from the fact that, while we can theoretically slap -*ly* onto most any adjective or participle to turn it into an adverb, in many instances we don't for aural reasons. You could write *misinformedly* or *mangledly*, but these words do not come trippingly off the tongue. The trick is to avoid erring in the opposite direction.

* * *

Although modifiers are far less problematic than some other elements of our writing, there is no question that they can be tricky. In our texts, we can find it extremely difficult to know when we've gone far enough. The only fair advice: Describe what you want in total and loving detail, and then be brutal with yourself. Hack and hew. Let your casual readers and editors be your guide. If they want more, they will tell you. If they are bored, take that into account. As the author, you need to know far more than your reader does. The fact that Laurie's purse is brown pigskin may be significant to you in conceiving Laurie, but it can be entirely meaningless in the larger context of your story. These characters—in fiction or nonfiction—belong to you and are real to you in a way they will never quite be to those who read your work, no matter how deeply they are involved in your narrative. Try as we might as authors, we cannot make these products of our pasts or imaginations quite so vivid via the medium of language as they are to us. What we create is a simulacrum of these Platonic visions of people and places and events.

But, hey, that is what Charles Dickens did with Scrooge; what Gabriel García Márquez did with the village of Macondo; what Stephen Crane did with the Civil War.

We could do a lot worse.

4

Conjunctions and Prepositions

DEFINITIONS

As parts of speech, conjunctions and prepositions practice truth in advertising. **Conjunctions** "conjoin" elements in sentences and indicate those elements' relationship. **Prepositions** are "pre-positioned" in a phrase; that is, they appear first and signal that some kind of clarification or description of the words they modify is upcoming. As with adjectives and adverbs, these two parts of speech are generally straightfoward and well understood by writers, but each has built-in traps.

CONJUNCTIONS

With conjunctions, writers most frequently trip when they fail to recognize words that function conjunctively. We all know that *and, but,* and *or* are conjunctions, but we do not necessarily recognize some others—*for* and *before,* for example. The four different kinds of conjunctions are **coordinating, correlative,** and **subordinating conjunctions** and **conjunctive adverbs**.

Coordinating Conjunctions

The coordinating conjunctions are the most familiar ones. They join words, phrases, or clauses that have identical functions (subject, object, modifier, and so on). There are eight of these: *and, but, for, nor, plus, or, so,* and *yet.* Be careful, because some of these words function primarily as other parts of speech. *And* or *but* you recognize as conjunctions, but *for* and *plus* usually appear as prepositions, and *so* is often an adverb. Note the following examples:

> As always, Ellen left late, for she could never get her makeup just the way she wanted.
> ____

Billy called to say he had to work, so I went to the concert alone.

She had lied, yet Rob somehow forgave her.

Five of the conjunctions (*and, but, or, nor, yet*) connect words, phrases, or clauses, while *plus* can only connect words or phrases. The remaining two (*for, so*) connect clauses only.

She was pleasant yet wary.

Rain, cold, plus the worst migraine headache she had ever had made Jeannette wish she'd never gotten out of bed.

Paul didn't listen, so she went on her way.

Correlative Conjunctions

Correlative conjunctions function like coordinating ones, but they come in pairs. The ones that immediately come to mind are *either . . . or* and *neither . . . nor*, but this category also includes *not only . . . but also* and *whether . . . or*.

Either Pam stops her gossiping, or I'm going to do it for her!

Not only is that incorrect, but it's calumnious also!

Whether or not she understands is beside the point.

Subordinating Conjunctions

Subordinating conjunctions are quite numerous, though among the most common are *after, although, as, because, before, if, since, so, than, unless, when,* and *where*. We think of subordinating conjunctions as links between dependent clauses and independent ones, though the conjunction itself is what makes a clause dependent. With their coordinating conjunction, both clauses in the following sentence are independent.

Bernice played the oboe, and Frank was in the garage.

If, however, you substitute a subordinating conjunction for that *and*, then "Frank was in the garage" becomes a dependent clause.

> Bernice played the piano if Frank was in the garage.

Here are a few more examples of subordinating conjunctions at work.

> Rick went by the store after school closed.
> ___

> Unless you have a compelling reason, don't tell her.
> ___

> He never calls when her mother is at home.

Conjunctive Adverbs

If you think there are a lot of subordinating conjunctions, the number of conjunctive adverbs will floor you. They include *also, besides, consequently, furthermore, however, indeed, likewise, moreover, next, otherwise, still, then,* and *thus.* A conjunctive adverb can function in a sentence as both an adverb that modifies the clause it introduces and as the conjunction that links the two independent clauses of the sentence.

> Our journey was arduous and dull; however, we managed to keep our spirits up through song and the excessive consumption of Andrea's cognac.
> ___

> Jocelyn refrained from mentioning the incident; indeed, she almost forgot it herself.

Note that the conjunctive adverbs in these sentences are preceded by semicolons rather than commas. Commas alone would create run-on sentences, though they would be perfectly adequate if a coordinating conjunction appeared as well as the conjunctive adverb.

> Jocelyn refrained from mentioning the incident, and, indeed, she almost forgot it herself.

Beginning a Sentence With a Conjunction

And there's one more thing!

You have certainly heard this old rule: You cannot begin a sentence with a conjunction because the very presence of the conjunction indicates that a preceding clause ought to be connected.

The reality is, however, that writers have been beginning sentences with conjunctions for centuries. Indeed, if the initial word is a coordinating conjunction such as *and* or *but*, then what follows it is actually considered a grammatical sentence. If another kind of conjunction appears at the beginning, then the group of words is a sentence fragment, but writers employ fragments of one kind or another quite frequently. Regardless, in creative work, this structure is not at all unusual. In dialogue, for example, readers wouldn't bat an eye at

> "I know exactly what you're talking about," Phillip said.
> "And what might that be?"

or

> "I mean, nobody gives a damn," Reggie spat.
> Dwayne pulled himself up to his full height. "Besides the people who lost their shirts in the bankruptcy."

In narrative, the reason to start a thought with a conjunction is usually to emphasize the words that come after it.

> She could tattle, of course. But who really needed to know?
> ——
> Lanie was convinced Jan was out to get her. And who wouldn't be!
> ——
> It was almost too easy. If, of course, Aaron remained in the dark about the plot.

Essentially, when you do start a sentence with a conjunction you should be aware of what you are doing and why. Don't overuse this structure: doing so every third sentence undermines its impact.

PREPOSITIONS

A preposition establishes the relationship between its object (a noun or pronoun) and the word that it is modifying. That is an extremely significant role to play in a sentence. Take a look at the following and how the simple change of preposition entirely alters the meaning of the sentence.

John fought about the tiger.

_____

John fought against the tiger.

_____

John fought beside the tiger.

_____

John fought despite the tiger.

_____

John fought like the tiger.

_____

John fought over the tiger.

_____

John fought past the tiger.

_____

John fought toward the tiger.

_____

John fought with the tiger.

On the whole, you may be comfortable with this part of speech, but be aware of some areas where problems arise.

Prepositions, Verbs, and Idioms

Writers sometimes stumble when employing more than one verb, which idiomatically requires a particular preposition to make sense. These are not, by the way, **particle verbs**; that is, root verbs whose meaning is changed by the addition of a prepositional component (_take on, take out, take over, take up_). These verbs simply are always followed (not necessarily immediately) by a particular preposition that is appropriate to the meaning of the verb itself.

This sounds more complicated than it is. Look at the following example:

Annie differed from her brother, Tom.

———

Annie differed with her brother, Tom.

The first sentence indicates that Annie and Tom were distinct in terms of personality, appearance, character, or some other individual quality. The second says that Annie and Tom disagreed about something. These kinds of idiomatic usage simply have to be learned.

Idioms are sometimes confusing, especially as you move among different parts of speech. When you change from *differ* to *different*, the commonly accompanying preposition becomes *from*, not *with*. To further illustrate, someone or something can have a "relationship to" or a "relationship with" someone or something else, and the meanings of these are notably distinct.

My relationship to Lucia is unclear.

———

My relationship with Lucia is unclear.

The first of these implies that the narrator has some familial connection to Lucia either by blood or marriage, though he doesn't know precisely what it is. The second indicates that there is some sort of personal connection (a romantic involvement, a friendship) shared by Lucia and the narrator, but its exact nature is indeterminate.

Now back to those idiomatic verbs. What's wrong with this picture?

The new text differed and yet related to Godfrey's earlier work.

The problem here resides in the sentence's compound verb. Godfrey's new text is both distinct from and yet similar to others he has produced. In the rendition above, however, *differed* drifts in the sentence, its meaning unclear. The sense of *differ* is determined by the preposition that follows it. As we've noted, you "differ with" another person with whom you may "differ on" a particular topic. However, when compared, two people or objects or whatever "differ from" one another.

In the sentence above, Godfrey's text appears to "differ to" his earlier work, which makes no sense. To be correct, the sentence must also include the preposition that clarifies *differed*'s meaning, and that is *from* rather than *to*. *To* is the correct preposition attached to *related*.

The new text differed from and yet related to Godfrey's earlier work.

Ending a Sentence With a Preposition

Just as a supposed rule forbids you from starting a sentence with a conjunction, an even dumber one forbids ending a sentence with a preposition. Applying that rule to the prepositions that serve as the particles in particle verbs is absurd. You wouldn't write "Don't screw up it" in lieu of "Don't screw it up." Beyond this, there's little point in pretzeling your poor sentence just to avoid having a preposition at the end.

With whom do you differ?

_____

At what are you driving?

_____

It was apparent to whom she intended to give the prize.

All of these sound clunky and self-conscious compared to

Whom do you differ with?

_____

What are you driving at?

_____

It was apparent whom she intended to give the prize to.

This whole brouhaha arose a few centuries back when well-intentioned and totally misguided pedants attempted to impose the rules of Latin grammar on the English language. This was never a good idea. Sir Winston Churchill came up with perhaps the best and most ludicrous example of what this particular "rule" can lead to:

"This is the sort of English up with which I will not put."

Interjections

The **interjection** is one other part of speech, though often we don't even think of it as such. Interjections range from strong (*Damn!*) to mild (*My, my*), and also include those such as *ouch* or *wham* or *tsk-tsk*. Writers usually handle these with no problem, and the primary admonition with regard to interjections is to avoid overusing them. The "soft" ones (*well, goodness, gosh*) can get distracting in dialogue if they come up too often. They draw attention to themselves after a while and appear to be some kind of authorial crutch. It's true that many people depend on these words or phrases—*ya know* or *as I say* or *um* to get them through a complete thought. We may tune these out when we're talking with somebody, but we do notice them when they appear in print.

With expletives (*Hell!*) or onomatopoeic words (*Bam!* or *splash*), the same phenomenon occurs. Too many of these make a story read like something from the funny papers.

Note that interjections are always set off by some kind of punctuation. This can be an exclamation point, a period, a comma, or dashes. Something always separates it from the main body of the sentence.

Slam! Cory was gone before she knew it.

———

Oh, golly, whatever are we going to do?

———

She heard it again—hmmmm—like a refrigerator that needed adjusting.

Perhaps the most interesting thing about interjections is that they exist as an independent category. Their function within the language is indescribable under the rubric of any other part of speech.

Sentences and Paragraphs

In the introduction to this part of the book, I made reference to a song from Rogers and Hammerstein's *The Sound of Music,* "Do-Re-Mi." Let's now move on to a song from a later and more sophisticated musical comedy, Stephan Sondheim's *Saturday in the Park With George*: "Putting It Together." In the end, stringing all those words and phrases and clauses to one another is what writers do. Words and phrases in isolation don't get us anywhere. They have to be hooked to one another to make sentences, and those sentences need to be grouped into paragraphs in order for us to communicate what we want to say.

Again, let's assume that you're fairly knowledgeable about sentences, first of all that they come in four kinds: **simple, compound, complex,** and **compound-complex**—all of which I'll cover in this chapter.

SIMPLE SENTENCES

A simple sentence is one made up of a subject and a verb; it has a single independent clause.

LuAnne plays.

———

Sit!

As you can see, in the imperative mode, a sentence can consist of one word because the subject (*you*) is understood.

Simplicity, however, can get a little complicated. A simple sentence can also include objects and indirect objects of the verb, complements of the subject, and all the modifiers of these—adjectives, adverbs, prepositional phrases.

LuAnne played the piano.

———

LuAnne played Ron her favorite sonata.

———

Dressed entirely in black, LuAnne from Pea Ridge played big-city boy Ron her favorite Beethoven sonata.

Further, subjects or objects in a simple sentence can themselves be compound.

LuAnne and Edith played Ron and Ellery their favorite Beethoven duet.

———

In return, Ron and Ellery played and sang LuAnne and Edith the famous duet from *The Pearl Fishers.*

In the final example I'd be inclined to include *to* before "LuAnne and Edith," though the sentence is perfectly correct as it is.

COMPOUND SENTENCES

A compound sentence, unsurprisingly, is made up of two or more independent clauses joined sometimes by one or more coordinating conjunctions (see chapter four). If the sentence has more than two clauses, they are generally separated by commas, and the conjunction appears at the beginning of the final clause. When the clauses are particularly long or complex, semicolons rather than commas separate them.

LuAnne played piano, Ron sang, and Edith danced with Ellery.

———

Breathless, LuAnne played the piano with astonishing fervor; flushed and excited, Ron sang as if possessed; and Edith, overwhelmed by a passion she had never felt before, danced wildly with Ellery.

COMPLEX SENTENCES

A complex sentence, seems more complex than simple or compound ones because it includes one independent clause and one or more dependent clauses. Indeed, the preceding sentence is a complex one: The clause following *because* is dependent upon the independent clause. This kind of dependency or **subordination** can be signaled by subordinating conjunctions, conjunctive adverbs, or relative pronouns.

Don't get scared. You know from the discussions in earlier chapters what those words or phrases mean. Check out the following examples:

> While Edith and Ellery took a break, LuAnne played the piano, although Ron really wanted to.

The only independent clause in that sentence is "LuAnne played the piano." The other two clauses are subordinate. Note, however, that if the subordinating elements (*while, although*) were removed, those clauses could stand as independent clauses, or even as sentences.

> Edith and Ellery took a break. LuAnne played the piano. Ron really wanted to.

COMPOUND-COMPLEX SENTENCES

This is a hybrid of the compound and complex sentence structures. A compound-complex sentence includes multiple independent clauses and at least one dependent clause.

> Edith and Ellery took a break, and LuAnne played the piano, although Ron really wanted to.

Now that we've reviewed the various structures of sentences, let's move on to the kinds of problems creative writers often face in this area.

PROBLEMS WITH SENTENCES
Run-On Sentences

Beware of run-on sentences. Such a sentence is often a jumble of clauses that beg for punctuation.

Eddie was smart everyone said so it was simply the truth.

The three independent clauses in this example are merely strung together without really being connected. You could add some subordinating elements, rearrange some words, drop the *so*, and make a somewhat clunky compound-complex sentence out of this.

Everyone said that Eddie was smart, because it was simply the truth.

That doesn't say quite the same thing, however. Why not just let the simple sentences be simple sentences?

Eddie was smart. Everyone said so. It was simply the truth.

The three clauses separated by periods make sense without any question as to meaning. This points up that there is nothing wrong with a three- or four-word sentence if it says what it has to say.

More often, run-ons result when the writer tries to pack too much disparate information into a single sentence.

Eddie was the most popular boy in school because he was really smart and also good looking and was so athletic that he was captain of the cross-country team, the hockey team, and the track team that won the state championship last year.

Here, the author tries to write *All About Eddie* in one sentence using conjunctions to link together clauses that concern a range of Eddie's qualities and accomplishments. Among other problems, the sentence is *wordy*. The recurrent forms of the verb *to be* throughout indicates some needless repetition. The sentence begs to be either broken up or reworked so it will be both more complex and more succinct. A writer could accomplish this in a number of ways; here are two examples.

Eddie was the most popular boy in school. He was smart, good looking, and so athletic he captained the cross-country team, the hockey team, and the track team that won last year's state championship.

———

Eddie was the most popular boy in school: smart, good looking, and so athletic he was captain of the cross-country team, the hockey team, and last year's state champion track team.

Bear in mind that, in creative work, questions of "running on" do not always have cut-and-dried answers. In the work of certain writers, particularly Modernists, it was simply the rule. All convention was laid aside, especially in instances of, say, interior monologues, so that the words flowed after one another in what was a literary attempt to capture the process of thought and dream.

If you have made that aesthetic choice, go for it.

However, most current prose does not overtly imitate that of William Faulkner or Virginia Woolf. Keep an eye on your more elaborate compound and compound-complex sentences. Be sure that the relationships among the elements in them are clear and not needlessly complicated. Keep the prose streamlined so that your reader can proceed smoothly through your story.

Choppiness

You can, of course, err in the opposite direction. Too many short simple sentences in a row can make your story sound amateurish or dumbed down.

It was a beautiful day. Kayla was so excited. She would meet her cousin Carolina today. Carolina was from Mexico. She was Kayla's mother's sister's daughter. They had never had enough money to bring her to the States.

This sounds as if the last book the writer read was *Fun With Dick and Jane*. Play just a little with structure, though, and these become perfectly functional introductory sentences.

It was a beautiful day, and Kayla was excited. Today, she would meet her cousin Carolina from Mexico, the daughter of her mother's sister. Never before had they had enough money to bring her to the States.

Varying Syntax

Choppiness usually results from a lack of variation in **syntax**. In English, the syntax—the order in which words fall—of a sentence is incredibly important. Other languages have features—distinctive suffixes or prefixes, gendered nouns (that is, everything is either masculine or feminine)—that allow scrambling sentences every which way without clouding which words are linked to others and how. Writers who use English must work harder to prevent muddled meaning due to shuffled words whose interrelationships are no longer apparent. However, to avoid phenomena such as choppiness, writers must also make sure all the sentences in a paragraph don't repeat the same syntax.

> LaVonne walked out the door on her way to the market. She was a pretty girl with hennaed hair. She had beautiful almond-shaped eyes, had a good figure, and knew how to dress well. She knew she was very pretty.

Each of these sentences is structured almost identically. Compare that paragraph to the following one:

> LaVonne walked out the door on her way to the market. With her hennaed hair and almond-shaped eyes, anyone who saw her would call her beautiful. Of course, she watched her figure and had good fashion sense. She knew she was pretty.

The second version has a nice balance—two sentences that employ introductory prepositional phrases (one adjectival, one adverbial) framed by two simple sentences. With the paragraph composed in this manner, a certain weight gets thrown onto what we assume is the most significant fact revealed here—LaVonne is *aware* that she's pretty.

Don't think that more-experienced authors are immune from the problem of repetitive syntax. Certain patterns characterize our individual styles of speaking and writing. I myself favor some kind of introductory gesture in sentences; this means that when I finish a rough draft I have to reread the text and watch out for those five sentences in a row that begin with a prepositional phrase or an adverb set off by a comma. It's essential to go back and make sure that your syntax is identical from sentence to sentence only when that is what you intend.

ANTECEDENTS

A common syntactical problem arises from how modifiers and phrases relate to other words in a sentence. In the following example, the sentence suffers from vagueness:

> When she was ten, Linda's sister Faye told her she had been adopted.

Who was ten at the time of this revelation? Was Linda the adopted child, or was Faye adopted? It's not clear which noun each of those *shes* refers to. The only way to deal with this is to recast the sentence. For example:

> Linda, when she was ten years old, was told about her adoption by her sister Faye.

It might seem this makes apparent that Linda was the adopted child and was ten years old when she found out about this fact from her sister. However, the sentence can also be read to say Linda's sister was the person who adopted Linda.

In the end, maybe the sentence should be constructed as follows:

> When Linda was ten, her sister Faye revealed to her how, some years before, she had discovered that Linda was adopted.

Here, at least, we know who was ten and who was adopted. Still, we have to throw in the towel with those pronouns and repeat Linda's name in order for the sentence to read clearly.

In instances such as this, you may need a more drastic revision.

> Linda's sister Faye sat her down. She told her that, ten years before, their parents had gone to the orphanage, picked up Linda, and brought her home.

> When Linda was ten, her sister Faye blurted out to her, "You were adopted!"

Parallel Structures

It is common in English, especially in creative work, to employ parallel structures in a sentence to lend it a certain rhythm and elegance.

He aspired to better things, to finer thoughts, to purer loves.

This is a stylistic device, and, traditionally, once you established the pattern of your parallel components you are stuck with it. In other words, you *don't* vary your syntax. For parallel structure, you wouldn't write " . . . to better things, to finer thoughts, and falling in love," though you could get away with "and to falling in love."

Creative writers, however, play a little faster and looser in prose than journalists or scholars can. A creative writer might draft the following sentence, which, strictly speaking, violates the stylistic norm:

They came from Michigan, from Iowa, from Texas and Florida and Vermont.

The conventional form would be one of the following:

They came from Michigan, from Iowa, from Texas, from Florida, and from Vermont.

——

They came from Michigan, Iowa, Texas, Florida, and Vermont.

To follow the "rules," you decide whether you are going to repeat that preposition or not; once you make that choice, you're committed. The five objects are all states and all coequal, so all share a single *from* or each gets its own.

Still, I think you'll agree that the first example has a panache that the other two lack. There is a certain poetic rush at the end as those state names tumble after each other, and that rush is achieved by violating conventional usage.

This is another artistic decision writers have to make. The pace and cadence of the prose and the characteristics of the narrator help make this determination.

Sentence Fragments

Sentence fragments are perfectly okay in creative works, as long as you as author know that's what they are. A sentence is constituted by *at least* a verb. "Stop!" is a sentence. However, verbless clauses or phrases may appear, as well as subordinate clauses that supposedly shouldn't stand alone. These are common in dialogue and as a means of adding emphasis. In the example below, the fragments are *italicized.*

> "She's gone to Memphis."
> *"To Memphis?"*
> Lorrie had a stunned look on her face. *Stunned and sad.* But there was nothing she could do to change things.
> "She'll be happier," Dan said softly. He took her arm. *"With him."*
> Lorrie pulled away violently. *"If he don't up and leave her!"*

Be sure you know when you're using fragments, and don't overdo it! Too many fragments might suggest that you aren't sure what a sentence is, and they can lend a choppiness that you generally want to avoid to the prose.

PARAGRAPHS

Much of our discussion regarding sentences carries over into the larger unit of prose: the paragraph. Writers need to keep an eye out for, among other things, both run-on paragraphs and choppy ones. The former tend to arise when a writer is really cooking in an extended narrative passage. There is nothing necessarily wrong with a paragraph that runs unbroken for an entire printed page, but this does raise a red flag, especially if it occurs over and over. Should you notice a page with nary an indentation in sight, see if the single paragraph could be divided into two. Nine times out of ten, this is the case. Don't break things up arbitrarily; look for some sort of shift in subject, however subtle, that justifies the division. If nothing else, this makes for less-intimidating text that your readers can get into more easily.

Conversely, if you find yourself with a sequence of paragraphs of only a line or two, take a minute to analyze what you're trying to accomplish. "Breaking paragraph"—that is, setting what might simply be the logical last line of a paragraph in a paragraph of its own—can effectively emphasize a particular moment in your story. However, if you do this all the time, then the device loses its punch. It can give the text a breathless quality that seems either silly or manipulative. The exception to this, of course, is in dialogue, when each speaker's utterance appears as a separate paragraph, no matter how short.

"I'm going."
"Please don't!"
"Sorry."

Your sentences and paragraphs determine how your work will be received. You may have a terrific plot, great characters, snappy dialogue, and so on, but if your prose doesn't work line by line, then all those other virtues are for naught. Although this sounds silly, take time to read your work aloud—every word. Listen. Always listen for spots where the syntax is repeated, for vague antecedents, for free-floating modifiers, for passive voice, and so on. Your readers will "hear" your sentences as their eyes move across the page. You owe them the best prose you can muster.

7

Capitalization

As in most languages, the rules of capitalization in English can seem eccentric. Just as an example, we write with an uppercase initial letter the days of the week, the months, and the names of holidays, but a day's date and a year are rendered in lowercase. Seasons are lowercased as well, except when they are being invoked, personified, or used as part of a place name. We do capitalize the name of a century when used as a noun, though this practice is changing.

Confused? Read the following illustration:

> There in darkest winter, still full of Christmas cheer, on the thirty-first of December of nineteen ninety-nine, a Friday, many people thought they were living the last day of the Twentieth Century.
>
> All Tony was thinking, there in the Winter Garden facing the Mississippi, was: "O Spring, please get your butt in gear!"

At least there is some consistency in what we capitalize and what we don't. Notions of what is worthy of uppercase and what should remain in lowercase evolve over time, with a tendency to "demote" words from the former to the latter. Here is a passage from a story in Rudyard Kipling's *Soldiers Three*:

> The barracks had the rumor almost before the Mess-room, and of all the nine hundred men in the barracks, not ten had seen a shot fired in anger. The Colonel had, twenty years ago, assisted at a Frontier expedition; one of the Majors had seen service at the Cape; A confirmed deserter

in E Company had helped to clear streets in Ireland; but that was all. The Regiment had been put by for many years.

Some of those internal capitals we would retain today—"the Cape" (as in that of Good Hope in Africa), "E Company" (a specific and titled unit of soldiers), "Ireland." You might be able to make a case for "Colonel" because the title is standing stead for a specific individual's name, though many writers would drop the initial letter to lowercase. "Frontier," assuming that in Kipling's context this represents for his characters a specific place, might also retain its capital. We would not, however, capitalize "Mess-room" or "Regiment." They are simply too generic to warrant a capital letter. Regiment—though it does refer to a specific larger unit in the army—is not a formal title as "E Company" is. We would capitalize, for example, "the Highland Regiment" and "the IVth Regiment." "Majors" would not be capitalized in that the referent lacks specificity.

Let's look at those instances in contemporary usage where we do capitalize.

CAPITALS WITH TERMINAL PUNCTUATION AND COLONS

As we all know, the first word of a sentence is capitalized, as is that of a sentence fragment that follows something ending with a period, exclamation point, or question mark.

He finally walked to the store. Meanwhile, Katie puttered around the house, trying not to fret about when they could afford to get the car fixed.

———

Fatefully, Eleanor knew she wanted Burton more than anything in the world. But could she have him?

———

There could be no other answer. Tuberculosis.

———

"Are you coming or not? Hurry up! We're going to miss the train!"

A capital can also appear after a colon if it is the first letter of a word that begins a complete sentence, the sense of which is not merely an expansion of what has previously appeared.

Millicent smiled as she watched Zack at work: What a piece of work is man, indeed!

Otherwise, use lowercase.

Millicent thought about her life: easy, quiet, lonely.

This holds true as well when you're merely illustrating or enumerating what you have already stated, even when you express that as a complete sentence . . .

Her life was not the problem: it was easy and quiet.

. . . though I'd be inclined in most instances like this to make the elements two sentences and be done with it.

Her life was not the problem. It was easy and quiet.

A capital letter may be appropriate with a sentence fragment or merely for emphasis.

Millicent smiled as she watched Zack at work: What a hunk!
_____

One word crossed Millicent's mind as she watched Zack at work: *Hunk*!

Take note of the *cans* and *mays* in this subsection. These are not hard-and-fast rules but rather issues of style, and these may differ greatly from writer to writer and publisher to publisher.

CAPITALS WITH OTHER FORMS OF WRITING

When you quote something such as the Kipling passage cited on page 63, you do not "correct" the capitalization to bring it into accord with contemporary conventions. Similarly, you do not do so with other kinds of writing. Should you have a character read or write a letter, follow the rules employed in that particular form. For example, capitalize the salutation in a letter—"Dear Sir," "My Dearest Sister," and so on.

With poetry, all bets are off. The poet determines what gets capitalized and what doesn't. When you include poetry in your text, the capitalization will depend on what poet is being quoted or what kind of poem your character is writing. Don't correct e.e. cummings or Walt Whitman!

> In his head, he heard the echo of Tennyson: "Half-a-league, half-a-league, half-a-league onward/All into the valley of death rode the six hundred."

———

> Looking at his dad, he thought of cummings:
> *my father moved through cooms of love*
> *through sames of am through haves of give,*
> *singing each morning out of each night*
> *my father moved through depths of height . . .*

CAPITALS WITH PROPER NOUNS

Proper nouns (e.g., "Randy," "Alicia," "Goethe," "Stravinsky," "Arizona," "Sri Lanka," "Republicans," "Methodist," "Portuguese," "Bantu," "General Motors," "the United Nations High Commissioner for Human Rights," "the Congress of the United States") are capitalized, as are adjectives derived from proper nouns ("Episcopalian ritual," "Italian cooking," "Wagnerian cadences," and so on). Exceptions to the latter rule have arisen because, as a consequence of longtime usage, we no longer associate a word with its place of origin: "french curve," for example. If you're uncertain as to what the contemporary consensus is, consult a current dictionary.

Races and ethnic groups or nationalities are capitalized ("Negro," "Dominican," "Polynesian," "Caucasian peoples"), though opinion differs on whether racial color should be written in upper- or lowercase. Generally, convention favors lowercase.

> Relations between Negroes and Caucasians were strained.

———

> Relations between blacks and whites were strained.

Unlike many other languages, English treats the **first-person pronoun**, *I*, like a proper name.

Oftentimes, I wish my wife would just lighten up a little.

Difficulties With Proper Nouns

Determining what constitutes a proper name can sometimes get a little tricky. Look at the following:

Boris became a captain in the U.S. Navy.

———

Boris became a captain in the American navy.

To see the distinction, think of it this way: The navy of the United States of America officially calls itself "the U.S. Navy," so *Navy* is capitalized. The American navy is simply one navy among many (the Argentine navy, the Swiss navy, and so on). For a similar situation, check this out:

She was elected Speaker of the House of Representatives.

———

She was elected Speaker of the lower house.

When a name is composed of a multiple elements ("the House of Representatives"), all its significant elements are capitalized while generally, less-significant ones (e.g., articles, prepositions, and conjunctions) are not. Making this distinction can sometimes prove a little thorny, especially with those initial articles. If the article is always included in a name, then it too is capitalized ("The Tell-Tale Heart," *The Mysterious Mountain*). Bear in mind, particularly when you're dealing with foreign titles, that the article may not be part of the original name. It's the *Iliad* of Homer and the *David* of Michelangelo, but Victor Hugo's *Les Misérables* and Mozart's *Die Zauberflöte*. If you're not sure, get verification in a reference text.

Obviously, such issues of capitalization can be subtle. One test you might use is to determine whether a title can be employed adjectively without the article. With "The Tell-Tale Heart," for example, this would be impossible unless you were writing a kind of shorthand, while, at least conceivably, you could write

Senate pages were well respected, but House of Representatives ones were not.

Another example of this test:

The congregation of the First Baptist Church met temporarily in the school auditorium.

———

First Baptist Church congregants met temporarily in the school auditorium.

Of course, if you drop specifying elements, then the capitalization changes.

The Baptist church congregation met temporarily in the school auditorium.

This is not totally loopy. In the last instance, *church* modifies the noun *congregation*, and *Baptist*—a proper name of a particular Protestant denomination— modifies *church*. Nonetheless, the specificity of that church is not established— it might be any Baptist church. In the example above, however, "the First Baptist Church" is a singular and specific church, as are for example, the Cathedral of St. John the Divine or the Boston Avenue Presbyterian Church or Temple Beth Israel. In the first sentence of the example, *the First Baptist Church* functions as a proper noun that constitutes the object of the preposition *of*.

The second sentence of that example could also be written

Thanks to Mr. Logan, the First Baptist Church [or *Church's*] congregation met temporarily in the school auditorium.

Again, "First Baptist Church" is the proper name of a specific church and is capable, as an entity, of possessing its own specific congregation.

When you deal with names of organizations or companies, it is often wisest to simply imitate whatever capitalization the entity employs: For example, a store in your town may be called "The Federated," and a bank may be called "the Federated Mutual Bank." When all else fails, seek guidance in a reliable and relatively contemporary source—the phone directory, the newspaper, an advertisement by the company or organization—in which the name appears.

CAPITALS AND PEOPLE

Titles of individuals ("Reverend Smith," "Mr. Scott," "Mrs. Jones," "Miss Edwards," "Ms. Feinberg," "Doctor [or Dr.] Blake," "Detective Lansdowne," "Nurse Windsor," "Bishop Connor," "Princess Gilberta," "Congressman El-liot"), usually require capital letters.

This can get a shade complicated when the title stands alone. You need to consider whether the title is replacing a proper name or merely referring to an occupation or class of individuals.

> She turned to Lansdowne. "Well, what do you make of that, Detective?"
> The detective scratched his ear and said nothing.
>
> ———
>
> "Can one senator among one hundred make a difference? That's what you have to decide for yourself, Senator!"

When certain titles are used as generic nouns, they do not require a capital. Compare the following:

> "Time for your pill, Mr. Williams."
>
> ———
>
> He thought of how, over the years, Mr. John had been very good to him.

to

> "Hey, mister! Don't stand so close to that turbine!"

However, if you "invent" a name that includes a title, it is capitalized, even though it is not strictly a proper name.

> "That's quite enough out of you, Miss Priss!"
>
> ———
>
> When his dad found out, Mr. Smarty-Pants would be putting on quite a show for everybody!

Words of polite or respectful address are generally not capitalized.

"I'm very sorry to hear that, ma'am."

———

Sergeant Marshall snapped to attention. "Yes, sir!" he barked.

Nevertheless, honorific terms for officials are

"Your Eminence, that is not so."

———

"Thank you, Your Highness."

———

"I'd like to question that, Mr. President."

———

"No, Your Honor."

If a **number** is part of a name and title, it too is capitalized. In such instances, the use of Roman numerals is also appropriate.

She desperately wanted to meet Queen Elizabeth the Second.

———

She desperately wanted to meet Queen Elizabeth II.

When used without a possessive modifier (*my, their, Lou's*), terms of relationship are "titles."

"I told Mom I was going to the store."

———

"What do you mean, Sis?"

———

"I always adored Uncle Harry."

In these instances, the titles are replacing a proper name (*Mom* = Harriet Brown Turner; *Sis* = Paula).

However, if these words *are* modified with a possessive noun or pronoun, they are generic terms of relationship and are *not* capitalized.

"I told my mom about it."

"He didn't know what his sister meant."

"She never liked Dan's dad."

"I always adored my uncle Harry."

Note that the last sentence implies that the speaker has more than one uncle: *Harry* is not set off by a comma. As we'll discuss in chapter nine, inserting a comma between *uncle* and *Harry* implies that they are synonymous.

Confusion may arise when relationship terms are used to refer affectionately to friends or even recent acquaintances in the way we would use words like *guy* or *dear*. In such cases, these words are *not* capitalized, just as we do not capitalize most other endearments (*honey, sweetheart, babe,* and so on).

"Hey, bro, how's it going?"

"You rock, sister!"

"Don't you think so, stud muffin?"

"Hey, son, how's it going?"

These instances (with the exception of *stud muffin,* which is not yet an established family relationship) tell us that those being addressed are not, in fact, the biological or legal siblings or offspring of the people addressing them. Hence, if you write "What do you mean, Son?" or "I can't tell you, Dad," you indicate that the younger man is truly the offspring of the older one. Conversely, if you write "What do you mean, son?" you use *son* as merely an affectionate or conventional form of address for a boy or young man by someone older.

CAPITALS WITH PLACES AND REGIONS

The names of **places**—not merely countries, but states, provinces, cities, streets, parks, rivers, lakes, seas, oceans, mountain ranges, and so on—are capitalized, for example:

Maine   British Columbia

Tokyo	Michigan Avenue
the Ohio River	the Río de la Plata
the Caspian Sea	the Atlantic
the Gulf Coast	the Alps

While regions are usually capitalized, mere directions are not. Compare

Though a great patriot, his first loyalty was always to the South.

_____

In Vermont, her dreams were always of the West.

_____

His were solid, Midwestern virtues.

to

Head south, then make a turn to the east.

_____

She went west.

To adopt an image from Orwell, "some regions are more equal than others." Some have achieved the status of place names, while others have not.

Ironically, after his stint as a beach boy in Southern California, Anthony moved to the mountains of southern Bolivia.

_____

Babs was so totally East Coast that she was completely at sea on the Oregon coast. She had never lived anywhere but along the eastern seaboard.

This can get quite complicated. For example, Detroiters tend to identify themselves as "Eastsiders" or "Westsiders," depending on which side of Woodward Avenue they live on. Chicago is divided into the "North Side" and the "South Side" by Division Street. Certain New York neighborhoods are known as "the Upper West Side," "the Lower East Side," and so on.

If these kinds of designations are part of the common parlance, then they are capitalized. If they are merely descriptive, they are not.

She gave up looking for a cheap apartment on the East Side.

_____

He lived on the east side of town, right on the river.

Often, the proper name (e.g., "the Andes," "the Hudson," "the Mediterranean") stands alone, and hence the element related to it, unless immediately preceding or following the proper name, should not be capitalized. We write

Miriam spent the night in the valley of the Hudson.

but

Miriam spent the night in the Hudson Valley.

This practice is in flux, however. Some contemporary dictionaries now cite *Hudson valley* as preferable. Again, this may be an issue of house style. Unless a writer can come up with an exceptional reason to stick to her guns on a particular usage, it is easier to accede to the publisher's particular preferences.

In some instances, a term is a name or a part of a name; in others, it is merely descriptive.

In her hand, she held the Great Seal of the State of Kansas.

─────

The state of Kansas is immense.

─────

Ralph had always wanted to travel to the East.

─────

Ralph had always wanted to travel to the east.

In the first sentence about Ralph, assuming Ralph is an American, his implicit desire is to travel either to the Orient or to the Northeastern region of the United States. In the next sentence, assuming that Ralph lives in, say, Georgia, his desire is simply to go sniff around Savannah and its environs, as opposed to heading west toward Birmingham, Alabama.

At times you have to decide precisely how a term is being used—specifically or descriptively.

Xerxes moved to the North Side of Chicago, far over on the east side, facing the Lake.

In this instance, *Lake* is a kind of shorthand for "Lake Michigan." For

Chicagoans there is only one "real" lake, just as San Franciscans live in "the City" and know about a lot of other "cities." Nonetheless, if you intended simply to indicate that Xerxes rented an apartment that overlooked water, it would be acceptable to write

> Xerxes moved to the North Side of Chicago, far over on the east side, facing the lake.

Note as well here that *North Side* is capitalized and *east side* is not. This is because, as we've noted, Chicagoans divide their city into north and south rather than east and west.

What you mean for your characters to say is key in these cases, and, in the end, whether something is capitalized or not can seem merely arbitrary.

> In Pensacola, Lulu twiddled her toes in the Gulf and then continued on to Miami, where she waded into the ocean.

In this instance, had we written *Atlantic* rather than *ocean*, we would have capitalized it, just as we would *Atlantic Ocean*. Here *Gulf* (as in "Gulf of Mexico") is specific, whereas *ocean* is generic, even though we know that if Lulu's in Miami, she's wading specifically into the Atlantic Ocean rather than the Indian Ocean.

Go figure.

OTHER INSTANCES OF CAPITALIZATION

The words in titles of literary and other creative works, with the exception of internal articles, conjunctions, and prepositions, are capitalized (e.g., *Moby Dick, Women on the Verge of a Nervous Breakdown, The Rime of the Ancient Mariner, On Language, Peter Grimes,* "Stairway to Heaven," *The Burial of Count Ordaz,* Symphony no. 1 in D Minor).

Likewise, **eras and movements in art, literature, politics,** and **religion** are usually capitalized, as are **centuries if they are employed as nouns.**

> Victor Hugo, the greatest of the Romantic novelists, asserted the free-dom of the artist from passing political dictates.

Social conditions during the Renaissance varied from country to country.

———

Frustrated by his poverty, Luke was attracted to the No-Nothings.

———

At the end of the Twentieth Century, we thought that we lived at the end of history.

This last usage is one in transition, i.e., in the foregoing sentence, it would also be proper to write "twentieth century" in lowercase. This is always done when a specific century is employed as an adjective.

In the annals of twentieth-century debate, a nadir was reached when Senator Gorman physically attacked his opponent.

The **names of deities** begin with capital letters: "God," "Allah," "Krishna," "Isis," "Yahweh," and so on. Traditionally, pronouns replacing these names are also capitalized, though this often depends on whether or not the writer is a worshipper of the particular deity evoked.

In English, **academic subjects** are *not* capitalized.

Tom signed up for physics and physical education.

The exceptions to this are **languages, subjects with adjectives of nationality**, and **titles of specific courses**.

Sally studied Latin, and she was also an expert in French literature.

———

Tom signed up for Physics 302: "In Quest of Quarks" and Physical Education 105: "Badminton Basics."

THE QUESTION OF ALL CAPS

For the most part, using **ALL CAPS** for emphasis looks cheesy, more like a comic strip than a serious narrative. Depend instead on the strength of the words on the page and the occasional exclamation point to put across the intensity of what you express. Write

"You told him what!"
as opposed to
"You told him WHAT!"

If you're absolutely insistent on the need for greater emphasis, employ italics.

"You told him *what*!"

There are, admittedly, a few cases where all caps is appropriate. For example:

She stared at the headline in doomsday type: "WAR!"

I saw another example in a story presented in a workshop. The protagonist received a note "written in the heavy black scrawl of a magic marker: HELP ME!"

The text in the note was, like the headline, literally printed in capital letters.

Later in the story, as the hero retells all the problems he's facing, this appears once again:

Where was all this headed? Girlfriends who didn't sympathize and people dying like flies and militia drills down by the creek and unknown people demanding that he HELP them? What was he supposed to do?

All caps works in this specific case, though it isn't required. The presence of HELP, however, specifically reminds us of the note in a way lowercase would not, and it makes the passage funnier. Even though this is a paraphrase of the protagonist's thoughts, that HELP indicates to us precisely how he "hears" the word in his head.

* * *

As you can see, capitalization in English can be a little goofy, but it's not entirely arbitrary. The historical trend, as we've noted, is for fewer words to be capitalized, though it's unlikely that the names of people, places, or things such as works of art will be demoted to lowercase. It's wisest, if you're unsure whether to capitalize or not, to err conservatively and capitalize the word. A quick slash across the letter with an *lc* in the margin is all your editor needs to do to let a proper noun know that it's just become a commoner.

8

Plurals and Possessives

PLURALIZATION

If you think capitalization in English is screwy, think about how we change a singular to a plural. Many languages just slap an *s* onto the end of a word, and away we (or they, or you all) go. When we add an *s* to an English word, we're just getting started.

Adding s

Actually, the plurals of the vast majority of nouns in the English language are indeed formed by adding an *s*.

boys	medics
cops	photographs
elephants	sources
falconers	tarantellas
lentils	yews

Words Ending in *f* or *fe*

An exception to this occurs for pluralizing some but not all nouns ending in *f* or *fe*. In the exceptions, *f* or *fe* gets changed to *ve* before adding the *s*, for example:

knife	knives
loaf	loaves
wolf	wolves

But some words ending in *f* or *fe* merely take an *s* to form their plurals.

fief	fiefs

fife	fifes
puff	puffs

There is no rule to explain these differences. You simply have to learn these plurals on a word-by-word basis.

Adding es

If a word ends in *s, z, x, ch,* or *sh,* then you add *es* rather than just *s* to make the plural. This *is* a rule and always applies.

batches	lunches
bypasses	crashes
adzes	pluses
stashes	taxes
klutzes	watches

You can see the rationale for this. Adding an *s* to *bus* (the one you wait to ride on) transforms it into a different word, *buss,* which means "kiss." Adding an *s* to *buss* results in *busss,* which is essentially unpronounceable. The same kind of phonetic jumble would occur with *taxs* or *batchs.*

(If you're wondering, an *adz* is a sharp-edged tool used to dress wood, and it looks vaguely like a small pickax. Its major contemporary significance is as a high-scoring word in Scrabble.)

Words Ending in y

When words end in a *y* that is preceded by a consonant, the *y* gets changed to an *i* before and you add an *es.*

bellies	reveries
funnies	Tories
maladies	wallabies
opportunities	zanies

Words Ending in o

In cases where words end in *o,* things get muddy. For pluralization some of these take only an *s,* and some take *es.* Still others are completely unable to make up their minds and take one or the other depending on, at the time of pluralization, the phase of the moon, whether the month includes the letter *r*, or some other mysterious unknown factor.

autos	echoes	calicos *or* calicoes
bassos	heroes	lassos *or* lassoes
patios	tomatoes	tornados *or* tornadoes

Pluralization With Hyphens

Another class of nouns—**compound words**—is distinctive in pluralization. Compound words are often but not always hyphenated, and the significant element appears first and thus gets made plural. As you'll see, this isn't quite as esoteric as it may sound.

brother-in-arms	brothers-in-Christ
matron of honor	matrons of honor
father-in-law	fathers-in-law
passerby	passersby
knight-errant	knights-errant
Surgeon General	Surgeons General

Adding an *s* to the end of such a term is done only with an apostrophe in order to form the possessive.

son-in-law's [singular possessive]

sons-in-law's [plural possessive]

The Attorney General's position [singular possessive]

The Attorneys General's positions [plural possessive]

Other Applications of and Exceptions to These Rules

The rules enumerated so far apply not only to common nouns but to most, but not all, proper ones as well.

Browns	Lyttons
Perezes	Bettses
Joneses	Califanos
Hatches	Laushes
Petroskis	Saleses

To illustrate an exception:

All the various Bachs composed church music.

Though this is an exception, it is not illogical. The *ch* at the end of *Bach* functions not digraphically (as in *church*, for example), but as \k\. Adding an *es* to the end of *Bach* would transmute the hard sound of the German *ch* to the softer sound, as in *caches*, so English speakers would read the name as \bashes\ rather than \boks\.

By the way, these conventions are used also for the third-person singular forms of verbs in the present tense.

sights	hushes
hurls	coaxes
reverses	matches
flashes	possesses

Note, however, that with those *f* words (not to be confused with *the f* word), this does not hold true.

They ate like *wolves*.

———

She baked three *loaves* of bread for Burt.

but

Nancy always *wolfs* her food.

———

The way Burt *loafs* drives Trish crazy.

Congratulations, you've now completed the easy part.

Unusual, Archaic, and Foreign Pluralizations

Because English has complex and sometimes contradictory origins and is always pillaging other languages for words, we have a whole series of plurals that follow rules that don't strike us as English at all.

alumna	alumnae
alumnus	alumni
foot	feet
basis	bases
louse	lice

chapeau	chapeaux
man	men
child	children
medium	media
datum	data
tooth	teeth

My last statement was, obviously, ironic, in that some of the words just listed are among the most ancient our language has to offer—parts of the body, offspring, even humankind itself (with contemporary usage referring to males only). *Teeth, feet, women,* and *children* result from Old English rules of pluralization. It's interesting as well that, for our ancestors, mice and lice were apparently just an unremitting part of the daily routine, and those old plurals passed down from father to son to the present.

A number of the other words cited come from Latin or French and have simply never quite been naturalized. The first examples—*alumna, alumnus,* and the plural of each—are the feminine and masculine Latin words meaning "foster child" or "pupil." And, you must admit, *alumni* sounds a lot nicer than *alumnuses* would. Adding an *x* to form the plural of *chapeau* is merely the French convention, as forming the plurals of *datum* or *criterion* follows Latin ones.

Still, certain of these immigrants seem well on their way to obtaining their citizenship. Take *stadium* as an example of one that has already gotten its green card. While it's always correct to refer to more than one stadium as "stadia," most characters who are native speakers would probably use *stadiums,* except in instances where they were referring to structures dating from the ancient world.

Another naturalized form is *aquarium,* whose Latin plural is *aquaria.* In English, we now simply slap an *s* on the end to make *aquariums.*

One common error involving these irregular plurals is employing them as if they were singular. You've probably heard someone talk about "an alumni" of the local college. With some of these words, the usage may be changing simply because that's the way English works. Still, for the moment, that fellow is properly "an alumnus." Likewise, "data indicate" is correct, while "data indicates" is not. *Data* is plural, not singular.

Keep in mind, though, that only characters who are highly educated or interested in grammar would know the difference. If your narrator is a librarian, she would say "an alumnus"; if your narrator is a day laborer, he's more likely to say "an alumni," and these show how the language adopts and alters what is strictly correct according to its needs. Certain words have different plurals depending on how they are used. The correct plural of *stigma* is *stigmata*, but we use *stigmas* frequently because *stigmata* has become in the common language almost exclusively associated with Jesus' crucifixion wounds. When we speak of the organs of mass communication, we call them "the media," but when we talk about how goods are traded within cultures, we discuss "mediums of exchange." The same is true when we talk about fortune-tellers. It would be quite a sideshow indeed if it were full of geeks, bearded ladies, and "media" instead of mediums!

POSSESSION

You may be thinking, "Hey, why are we talking about plurals and possessives at the same time? One is a form of a noun or pronoun, while the other is a case, in the way of nominative and objective. All they have in common is the letter *s*." You're absolutely right. The reason to feature them back-to-back is simply that the two quite often cause confusion because of their common use of *s* in their formation.

Possessives, of course, indicate the relation of one thing to another: "Mary's book," "Tom's brother," "his car," and so on. The root of a possessive is a noun or pronoun, though the function of a possessive is most commonly adjectival.

In chapter one we considered the uses of and problems with possessive pronouns, so here we concentrate on nouns. Where nouns are concerned, possession is usually indicated by the addition of an apostrophe and an *s* (*'s*): "Emilia's shoes," "the officer's badge," "Randy's shirt."

Words Ending in s

Things get complicated when the word for the person or thing doing the possessing already ends with *s*. If the noun is singular, I'm inclined to add the *'s*: "Jesus's parables," "James's bitterness," "her relentlessness's impact." Nonetheless, some editors and organizations find it acceptable in these instances to add only the apostrophe: "Jesus' parables," and so on. If that's what your editor wants, then go with it. This is one of those instances where house style may differ.

If the noun is plural and ends in an *s*, then add only the apostrophe. The word resulting with the addition of yet another sibilant would be, at best, clumsy (e.g., "machines's.")

The Smiths' relationship to the Joneses' ancestors is unknown.

———

Americans' feelings about the war were gradually changing.

Again, house style may differ, and sometimes these, as well as your personal choices, may not be entirely consistent. An overarching element in your decision should be "euphony," which simply means "sweet sound" in Greek. Hence, I'd opt for "the sergeants at arms' sustenance." This is because the clot of sibilants in "sergeants at arms's" already seems almost comic, and with hissings of "sustenance" following, the phrase really does begin to sound like a snakes' nest. Nonetheless, some publications would, indeed, prefer "sergeants at arms's." We'll talk more about this whole issue in Part II, but bear in mind that the euphony in your prose is no insignificant matter.

Multiple Possession

If something is possessed by more than one person, then possessives are determined by whether that thing belongs to people individually or collectively.

I went by the apartment house and picked up Bob's and Cathy's mail.

———

I went by the apartment house and picked up Bob and Cathy's mail.

The first sentence implies that, though Bob and Cathy may inhabit the same apartment house or even the same apartment, they receive their mail individually—i.e., Bob and Cathy are probably not a couple, business associates, or the like. In the second sentence, "Bob and Cathy's" indicates that their mail is received collectively and leads us to believe that the two are related to one another in some sort of partnership. To further illustrate:

Theresa knew all the songs in Lerner and Loewe's *Camelot*.

———

Theresa learned that Lerner's and Loewe's estates were divided among multiple heirs.

––––

Among Austria-Hungary, Germany and Turkey's losses was their sense of being players on the world stage.

––––

Among Austria-Hungary's, Germany's, and Turkey's losses were the ports of Trieste, Danzig, and Beruit.

Lerner and Lowe jointly wrote *Camelot*, but their estates were separate. The three Central Powers collectively lost their sense of international significance, whereas each country lost control of a particular port it had individually controlled.

* * *

One final rule with regard to forming plurals and possessives: If you're unsure of what is correct, look it up.

That is why dictionaries are published.

That is why you own one.

9

Punctuation

Many writers have trouble with punctuation. There really is a logic to most English punctuation rules, though many of the "rules" can be somewhat elastic. Particular publications or institutions—*The New York Times*, the Modern Language Association, Random House, to name a few—establish their own norms of usage to which their writers and copyreaders are expected to conform. More important, however, writers themselves often find occasion to bend or break traditional rules and conventions in order to create particular effects in their prose.

To do this successfully, you need some notion of what the rules and conventions are. For too many apprentice writers, punctuation is an afterthought, but it is extraordinarily important on two levels—one aesthetic, the other practical. Question marks, dashes, ellipses, and so on are the means by which you assure that a sentence you write gets read the way you intended. There is much truth in this old saw: If words in prose function like the notes in music, punctuation marks are the rests. It would be impossible to play a Beethoven sonata or the Rolling Stones's "Sympathy for the Devil" without knowing where the rests fall. Likewise, reading even the simplest text without punctuation would be difficult, if not impossible.

To carry the musical image further, punctuation is the means we use to represent the intonations our voices provide when sentences are spoken, the volume and emphasis that give utterances their power. To cite a famous example: We read "Don't! Stop!" differently than we read "Don't. Stop." much less "Don't stop!"

An incorrectly or badly punctuated sentence invites multiple interpretations, some of which are bound to contradict the writer's meanings. Creative writers are artists, and while ambiguity may be a virtue in an overarching narrative, it can be deadly in a sentence. Be just as conscious of the punctuation you use as you are of the words you employ. Punctuation is an inherent part of style.

Happily, close to 90 percent of the time, the only marks of punctuation a writer needs are **periods** and **commas**—the first as "terminal punctuation," the other as "internal punctuation." This may seem boring, but it makes the whole issue of pointing a sentence a great deal easier.

TERMINAL PUNCTUATION: PERIODS, QUESTION MARKS, EXCLAMATION POINTS

Terminal punctuation are, obviously, the marks that usually end sentences. The vast majority of sentences end with a **period**. The reason for this is simple: Most of what we write or speak is simple declaration, and its mood is indicative.

> I'm going to the store.
>
> ―――
>
> Wanda's life ended tragically.
>
> ―――
>
> Japanese troops assaulted the island.

An exception occurs when a sentence, though indicative, is not a declaration but a question. Such a sentence may begin with a common interrogative word that may function as a pronoun, adjective, or adverb. Sentences of this type are usually punctuated with a **question mark**.

> What do you mean?
>
> ―――
>
> Why go that way?
>
> ―――
>
> Which one are you telling me about?

This is not always the case, however. You cannot assume, just because a sentence begins with *what* or *how*, that it will take a question mark rather than a period.

> Where she got the strength to do it, I don't know.
>
> ―――

What means you employ is entirely up to you.

——

Which choice he made would determine the outcome
of the contest.

The syntax of a sentence can also reveal its interrogative nature.

Is Tom going to the store with you?

——

Did Martha call?

——

Did Wanda's life end tragically?

Again, though, this isn't always the case. A writer can construct a sentence
as if it were a declaration and end the sentence with a question mark to indicate
that the thought is interrogative. Using this syntax, the questions in the previous example can be revised to read

Tom's going with you?

——

Martha called?

——

Wanda's life ended tragically?

Here, the punctuation alone determines how the sentence reads. This happens even more frequently with the other mark of terminal punctuation, the
exclamation point. You see it often when the mood of the sentence is imperative (a command).

Get down here!

——

Don't you talk to me like that!

——

Just play the game!

Once again, such sentences are often syntactically distinctive. In the first two examples, the subject of the sentence—*you*—is not stated. Imperatives can even consist of a single word.

> Run!

> ———

> Confess!

The exclamation point is also used for exclamations or interjections—words or phrases expressing emotions such as surprise, fear, or incredulity or imitating noises.

> Oh, no!

> ———

> My God!

> ———

> Wham! He hit me in the nose.

> ———

> He understood then the ship was sinking!

> ———

> The fuse was quickly consumed, and then . . . Ka-boom!

Certain verbs of utterance can automatically imply that the words spoken are exclamatory.

> "That was one stupid decision!" she wailed.

> ———

> Alma shouted, "Billy! The ice is too thin!"

> ———

> "Don't you ever say that!" he yelled.

A common error by apprentice writers is the overuse of the exclamation point. The more of them a writer employs, the less impact each mark has. Too many can make a text look breathless and overwrought.

> Lorna ran to the door! It was already open! The invaders were in the house! She screamed!

Oh, no! she thought. What am I going to do! "Help!"

The poor dear's really in a state, isn't she?

In a passage such as this, which exclamation points should stay and which should go? This is an authorial decision, but some logic applies. In that first paragraph, what is truly terrifying is that whatever danger is lurking is now in Lorna's house itself. Hence:

Lorna ran to the door. It was already open. The invaders were in the house! She screamed.

In the second paragraph, only the utterance deserves the exclamation point.

Oh, no, she thought. What am I going to do? "Help!"

In instances where a question is also an exclamation, the latter trumps the former.

"What are you talking about?" she asked.

———

"What the hell are you talking about!" she shrieked.

———

Was she crazy?

———

Was she crazy!

Do not under any circumstances employ the question mark and exclamation point together, as in "What?!" There was an attempt at one point to introduce a combination, called the "interrobang," which featured an exclamation point superimposed over a question mark (‽). Useful as this might appear, the idea never caught on.

One exclamation point or question mark suffices. Multiplying them makes a text look like that of a comic book.

"Could it be Batman???"

———

Slam! Bang!! Whomp!!!

Though question marks and exclamation points are generally terminal, they do occasionally appear as internal punctuation. In creative work, this most often occurs in a remark or commentary inserted parenthetically.

So, I decided I should apologize. I walked (!), bum leg and all, over to Sue's house and told her how sorry I was.

———

Lee went on about how bad he felt about the whole thing (I'm supposed to believe this?), scratching under his cast with a bent coat hanger while he spoke.

———

The whole time—and I mean the whole time!—she looked at me like I was some kind of bug.

This exception does not apply, however, with the period. Some obscure rhetorical rules govern these usages, but an easier explanation is that the period does not alter the quality or inflection of the words the way the question mark or exclamation point does.

He kept telling me he was drunk that night (I knew that) and I shouldn't take what he said seriously.

In a couple of peculiar instances, a period may appear midsentence. One is when a quoted sentence appears in the middle of another one. You saw an example of that in the introduction to this section on punctuation.

We read "Don't! Stop!" differently than we read "Don't. Stop." much less "Don't stop!"

"Don't. Stop." has to be quoted intact, including both periods.
This is probably something you will not confront when writing your memoirs.
A more common instance where a period is followed by another mark of punctuation, usually a comma, is when an abbreviation appears somewhere other than at the end of a sentence.

Working for Lincoln and Co., Mark learned the business inside out.

――――

"I told Sally she needed to work harder—i.e., she better get her butt in gear!"

Arguably, in creative work, this would be rare. In the first example, we might simply write out *Company* and be done with it. In the second, the appearance of such abbreviations as *i.e.* (shorthand for the Latin *id est*, "that is"), *e.g.* (*exempli gratia*, "for example"), and *etc. (et cetera*, "and so on") would presumably not pop up very often. Still, there's little way around inserting a comma after the period in the following:

As a vice-president at I.B.M., Lauren felt she had truly arrived.

However, many publications and publishing houses are now writing well-known abbreviations without periods ("IBM," "FBI," "IRS").

Writers have developed an odd aversion to periods, as if this most useful and significant punctuation mark were somehow boring and conventional. I receive from novices reams of stories that are plagued with ellipses and semicolons that appear for no apparent reason. If I ask for an explanation, the usual reply is, "Oh, I wanted to indicate there was a pause."

That is precisely what a period (and, in the appropriate circumstances, a question mark or exclamation point) does! A period denotes a full stop, as opposed to the slight pause signaled by, for example, a comma. Ninety-nine percent of your sentences will conclude with the three marks of terminal punctuation.

Ninety-five percent of those marks will be the humble and ever constant period.

INTERNAL PUNCTUATION: THE COMMAS

The **comma** has become the most abused, misused, misunderstood, bizarre, kinky, you-name-it mark of punctuation in the English language. In apprentice writers' stories, commas appear for no rhyme or reason, out of nowhere, and fail to appear where their use should be second nature to anyone who got past the third grade. This confusion may be the result of the comma's frequent employment in a wide variety of circumstances, as well as the elasticity of the rules governing its use. As you'll see throughout this section, though, the placement or absence of a comma is no small matter: It profoundly affects the way a sentence reads.

Comma Mistakes

To begin, let's look at how commas are misused. For reasons entirely obscure, some people think they must use a comma to separate the subject of a sentence from its verb. This generally is proper only when a nonrestrictive dependent clause of some kind falls between the two, as in

> My sister, who was out of town that day, used to go there quite often.
>
> ———
>
> The troops, unable either to retreat or to advance, dug in on the hillside.

You should *never* write

> My sister, used to go there quite often.
>
> ———
>
> The troops, dug in on the hillside.

These are rendered

> My sister used to go there quite often.
>
> ———
>
> The troops dug in on the hillside.

This is true even when the subject is followed by a prepositional phrase.

> One-third of the troops dug in on the hillside.

The same rule applies with a verb and its object, even when the object is a phrase or clause or when the verb is followed by a prepositional phrase.

> Laura indicated that she intended to quit.
>
> ———

Laura indicated to the entire office staff that she intended to quit.
But *never*

Laura indicated, that she intended to quit.

———

Laura indicated to the entire office staff, that she intended to quit.

Beware the dreaded **comma splice**. This occurs when a comma is employed instead of a semicolon or a comma plus a conjunction.

Yvette played the harpsichord, she was very good.

Wrong.

You can correct this in one of three ways: (1) change the comma to a semicolon, (2) insert a conjunction after the comma, or (3) break the sentence into two sentences.

Yvette played the harpsichord; she was very good.

———

Yvette played the harpsichord, and she was very good.

———

Yvette played the harpsichord. She was very good.

Serial Commas

Considerable confusion surrounds the most common and traditional use of a comma: separating elements in a series (hence, "serial"). Some current manuals of style demand that you separate each element with a comma, including the final element preceded by *and* or another coordinating conjunction, while others (such as that of *The New York Times*) do not. Depending on whose stylistics are being followed, either of the following can be correct:

She truly displayed faith, hope and charity.

———

She truly displayed faith, hope, and charity.

Regarding creative work, I'm of the opinion we should follow the more conservative rule, as illustrated in the second example—"faith, hope, and charity"—if for no other reason than that doing so allows us greater subtlety in our writing. Compare these two sentences.

> Kathy was sweet hearted, while Margaret was beautiful, proud, and sullen.
>
> ————
>
> Kathy was sweet hearted, while Margaret was beautiful, proud and sullen.

While these are both correct, there is a quiet but definite difference in the way we read them. In the first, "beautiful, proud, and sullen" are three characteristics of Margaret, and all are equally weighted, none more or less important than nor consequent of any of the others.

The second version hints at something more complex. Margaret's pride and sullenness are equated with each other. They are distinguished from her beauty, though they are, according to the sentence, implicitly a consequence of her beauty. You might argue that a dash would clear things up entirely ("Kathy was sweet hearted, while Margaret was beautiful—proud and sullen"), though it seems to me that this version also is distinct from the other two. The dash sets off the two qualities more radically than the comma does.

In sum, if you want elements in a series to be obviously equivalent, it is best to separate all of them, including the last, with commas.

SERIAL COMMAS IN LISTS

In any case, commas are used in lists of one kind or another to separate things in a series.

> Aaron Copland composed symphonies, ballets, concertos, film scores, and numerous pieces for solo instruments.

This is true even if the series consists of phrases or clauses.

> Mr. Elliot worked to improve relations between stockholders and company officers, to encourage good labor relations, and to present a friendly company face to the larger public.

In this latter example, you may recognize from chapter six that various phrases separated by commas are parallel; that is, they are identically structured and function identically in the sentence. It is worth repeating that, when you set up these sorts of series, you usually should maintain the identical structure throughout. In the illustration, each element is introduced by an infinitive: *to improve, to encourage, to present.* The following shows what you want to avoid:

> Mr. Elliot worked to improve relations between stockholders and company officers, to encourage good labor relations, and presenting a friendly company face to the larger public.

That present participle (*presenting*) comes clunking out of nowhere and ruins the parallel structure that was established.

Multiple Adjectives

With multiple adjectives, the use of commas is governed by which word or words are being modified. To come at it from a different direction, comma use depends on whether the adjectives in the series all have the same weight. Grammatically, the latter is what distinguishes **coordinate** and **noncoordinate** adjectives.

It's not quite so complicated as it sounds. Coordinate adjectives equally modify a noun.

> Bonnie turned to confront the loud, beefy drunk.

The drunk in question is both "loud" and "beefy," two separate and distinct qualities.

Now, look at this example.

> Bonnie's wine flew all over his new Armani suit.

Here *new* describes *Armani suit,* so a comma is not used after *new.*

Still perplexed? Relax, you have two ways to determine if you need to use a comma to separate adjectives modifying the same noun.

First, there's the "*and* test." Can you insert *and* between the adjectives? With *loud* and *beefy,* you can, so you need a comma. Would you do the same with *new* and *Armani*—"his new and Armani suit"? It sure doesn't seem like a good idea.

This particular tactic isn't foolproof, but you can use a second test to determine whether you should use one or more commas with a series of adjectives. This is the "reversal test." Can you alter the order of the adjectives and still have a sentence that communicates the same sense and sounds natural? With the first example, the answer is yes: A "beefy, loud drunk" is the same thing as a "loud, beefy drunk." Therefore, use a comma. However, with the second, "an Armani new suit" strikes the ear oddly and is almost nonsensical, so no comma is needed. When you're unsure, run both tests, and you should be okay with your commas.

Introductory Elements of Sentences

Commas separate **introductory exclamatories** (not all of which take exclamation points) and **expressions of affirmation or negation** from the rest of the sentence.

"Well, let's go!"

———

"Oh, who cares?"

———

"No, I don't want to attend."

———

"Oh, yes, I'd love to see her."

This is one of those areas that showcase elasticity vis-à-vis comma usage. Though opinions vary widely on this, I encourage the separation via a comma of *all* introductory elements, even if only a single word, from the body of a sentence. As you will see later in this section, this depends on precisely how you want the sentence to read, i.e., on its intended meaning and intonation. Still, unless you have a compelling reason not to, set off that initial element.

Finally, Sara arrived at the market.

———

Square and stout, Tom was the very image of the high school football player he had been.

———

Unable to either retreat or advance, the troops dug in on the hillside, taking advantage of the respite the storm provided from the assault.

The reason to separate by a comma these words or phrases is twofold. First, it simply makes the sentence easier to comprehend on the first reading. If you were reciting the sentence, you would normally pause briefly—take a breath—after "finally," "square and stout," and "unable to either retreat or advance." It would not be incorrect to write either of the first two sentences without a comma. The general rule is that an introductory phrase of more than four words must be separated from the body of the sentence, so the third sample sentence has kept its comma after the introductory element.

Second, a basic sentence begins with its subject ("Sara," "Tom," "the troops"). These three sample sentences start with modifiers. The first begins with an adverb (*finally*, which describes the verb *arrived* and tells us when Sara arrived), whereas the latter two begin with descriptive phrases. *Square* and *stout* are adjectives describing Tom; *unable to either retreat or advance* is an adjectival phrase describing the troops.

One test you can apply here is to ask whether the phrase in question absolutely has to be in its present position in order to read the sentence correctly or whether it could fall elsewhere.

Tom, square and stout, was the very image of the high school football player he had been.

————

The troops, unable to either retreat or advance, dug in on the hillside, taking advantage of the respite the storm provided from the assault.

Note that when each phrase is shifted to a later position in the sentence, it is set off with commas.

The example "Finally, Sara arrived at the market" can be treated a little differently, given the brevity of its introductory element. When rearranging the sentence, you would probably not set off *finally* with commas unless you wanted to emphasize that particular word. Hence:

Sara finally arrived at the market.

However, if you place the adverb after the verb, it might be a good idea to set it apart because it functions in a way that approaches the exclamatory.

> Sara arrived, finally, at the market.

We read this in a manner that almost (but not quite) carries the force of the following construction.

> Sara arrived—finally!—at the market.

If you employ an adverbial phrase rather than a single adverb (*finally*), set it off by commas.

> After a long and exhausting three hours, Sara arrived at the market.
> ———
> Sara, after a long and exhausting three hours, arrived at the market.

When the adverbial phrase falls after the verb, commas are not necessary. The two sequential prepositional phrases tell us where Sarah arrived and when Sarah arrived.

> Sarah arrived at the market after a long and exhausting three hours.

However, when a phrase interrupts the main clause of the sentence, even if it falls after the verb, it should be set off with commas.

> Sarah confronted, with heavy heart, the ruin that was her father.

Restrictive and Nonrestrictive Modifiers

Each of the examples in the previous section is **nonrestrictive**. In contrast, **restrictive** modifiers are *not* set off with commas.

So, what's the difference between restrictive and nonrestrictive modifiers?

In simplest terms, a restrictive modifier is essential for the proper comprehension of the sentence. The information it provides alters the nature of what it defines. Nonrestrictive modifiers, on the other hand, are basically descriptive.

They add information that does not absolutely, positively have to be there for us to understand what is being stated.

Note the difference between the clauses in these two sentences.

Cardiac surgeons, who can be a rather eccentric lot, pay very high malpractice insurance premiums.

——

Cardiac surgeons who make more than $250,000 a year pay very high malpractice insurance premiums.

The first sentence states that all cardiac surgeons pay high insurance premiums, and it suggests that all cardiac surgeons might be a shade eccentric. Any eccentricity of such doctors, however, is of secondary significance regarding the main clause of the sentence, which has to do with the insurance premiums.

The second sentence states that *only* cardiac surgeons making more than a certain amount of money per year pay high premiums. The clause beginning with *who* alters and restricts the subject of the sentence, so it is absolutely essential to correct comprehension. Hence, that clause is not set off by commas.

Writers used to be taught to distinguish between certain restrictive and nonrestrictive clauses by whether they were introduced by the restrictive pronoun *that* or the nonrestrictive pronoun *which*. This was kind of nice in that it obviated a lot of confusion about commas, though evidence that people ever strictly followed this rule is pretty slim.

Still, it's a useful notion that allows you to add subtlety to your expression.

The wooden clock that sits on the mantel belonged to my grandfather.

——

The wooden clock, which remained in its place on the mantel even during the earthquake, belonged to my grandfather.

The first sentence locates the clock in question and distinguishes it from any other clocks that happen to be nearby. The clause is restrictive because the information is essential to our awareness of which wooden clock we're talking about. In the second sentence, the nonrestrictive clause, set off by commas, provides interesting but inessential information about the clock.

APPOSITION

The easiest way to keep apposition straight may be to think in terms of essential vs. nonessential information. In the following two examples, simply the order of the words determines whether commas are employed.

The American novelist Mark Twain made several trips to Europe. ["Mark Twain" tells us which American novelist the sentence is about.]

———

Mark Twain, the American novelist, made several trips to Europe. [We don't need "the American novelist" to know which Mark Twain is being discussed.]

In the first sentence, setting off "Mark Twain" with commas would mean that America had produced only one novelist in its whole history, and he was Mark Twain. In the second sentence, however, "Mark Twain" does not need modification for recognition. The phrase "the American novelist" is inessential, so it is set off with commas.

This business of **apposition** can get quite subtle if you know what the rules are. In the following two sentences, the presence or absence of commas implies something about the structure of the family alluded to.

Mary's brother Mark took her to New Mexico.

———

Mary's brother, Mark, took her to New Mexico.

In the first sentence, the lack of commas indicates to us that Mark, rather than one of Mary's other brothers, took her to New Mexico. The second sentence, with *Mark* set off with commas, tells us that Mary has one brother and his name is Mark. The proper name merely restates "Mary's brother."

To cite another illustration:

My friend Ellen agreed with me.

———

My best friend, Ellen, agreed with me.

In the first case, *Ellen* tells us which of your countless friends agreed with you. In the second, on the assumption that a person can have only one best friend, *Ellen* simply repeats what is already stated. The friend's name is essential information in the first sentence and inessential information in the second sentence.

Compound Elements in Sentences

Except in a very short sentence, use a comma to separate two independent clauses joined by a conjunction. The comma falls before the conjunction.

The car careered off the road, and Lonnie was thrown across the backseat into the armrest.

———

The issue was never resolved, but many felt that Eleanor was the true culprit in the affair.
However,
Doris smirked and Nana wept.

When a sentence is composed of more than two independent clauses, use commas to separate the clauses if they function as elements within a series or if the clauses subsequent to the first one are introduced with coordinating conjunctions.

Marilee did the research, Tom composed the rough draft, Latisha polished the text, and Randall typed the final copy.

———

Tosca certainly had its moments as far as Jessie was concerned, and *Madama Butterfly* thrilled her, but *Turandot* was her favorite Puccini opera.

However, if neither of these conditions applies, then use semicolons to separate the clauses.

The city slept; Marco ranted; Esther continued her labors.

Don't forget that, though *and* and *but* are the most common, they are not the only coordinating conjunctions that can separate independent clauses. In some instances, *for, or, nor, yet, so,* and others can fulfill the same function.

> Blanche was often quiet, for she was deeply depressed about her mother's death.

———

> Don't get your hopes up, or you might be heading for a fall.

———

> Juan thought Barnaby seemed aloof, yet he couldn't help thinking about him every waking moment.

Don't forget that conjunctions such as *and* or *but* coordinate many things besides independent clauses. Don't insert commas where they are not needed. The following sentences illustrate proper omission of commas:

> The prose was very dense but not too difficult.

———

> The book was long and densely written.

———

> Ronald's consideration of the offer was colored by his own experience with girls and all the advice his friends so freely offered.

In this example, comma use is incorrect:

> The book was long, and densely written.

Unless there are more than two of them, compound objects or subject complements are not separated by commas. The same holds true for compound subjects and compound verbs if they consist of only two elements.

> The prose and the story's very plot represent Faulkner's experiments with Modernism.

———

> The characterization of Zeno had evolved and developed surprising nuances in Barbara's writing of the play.

———

> He produced numerous short stories but no novels until he was thirty-five years old.

If a compound subject, verb, or object has more than two elements, the elements should be separated with commas.

The prose, the characterizations, and the story's very plot represent Faulkner's experiments with Modernism.

Appended Adverbs

An adverb that falls at the conclusion of a sentence is set off with a comma, especially if it is separated from the verb it modifies.

Kathy wanted to go along with us, too.

――――

Her ideas were the same as mine, essentially.

Just as with the introductory elements we discussed earlier, these adverbs could "float"; that is, you could shift their positions without altering the sense of the sentences.

Essentially, her ideas were the same as mine.

――――

Her ideas were essentially the same as mine.

This last sentence could also correctly be written

Her ideas were, essentially, the same as mine.

Note that you read the sentence in a slightly different fashion when the adverb is set off with commas; that is, setting *essentially* between commas throws an emphasis onto the word that it lacks if it is merely integrated without pause into the sentence.

Asides and Direct Address

As you have probably noted by now, various "asides" (which are obviously inessential to the comprehension of a sentence) are set off by commas.

For example, Patricia never took drugs.

――――

Marilyn's characterization of the circumstances were, in fact, inaccurate and unfair.

———

That kind of whining, if you know what I mean, is simply unacceptable.

Too, words of direct address, whether proper names or general nouns, are set off by commas.

"Tom, can you come over here?"

———

"Larry, dude, it's great to see you!"

———

"Hey, guys, let's just split."

———

"I'm just tired of Toshi, man."

———

"Don't bother, Brady."

In the last instance, you can see just how important the comma can be. Were it not there, the meaning of the utterance would be altered entirely. Instead of telling Brady not to concern himself about something, "Don't bother Brady" tells somebody other than Brady to let Brady alone.

Commas and Tone

It should now be apparent that the comma is not some meaningless mark you stick into a sentence when it seems time to do so. It can control how the sentence gets read and what it means. This power also means that a number of the "rules" we have reviewed are not absolute. They can be overridden because of your intended meaning, the shadings and nuance you wish to convey or the intonation you would provide with your voice if you spoke the sentence aloud. This is of particular interest to creative writers. The following sentences show just how important it is to keep an eye on commas and, for that matter, all marks of punctuation.

"Now, what do you mean?" vs. "Now what do you mean?"

———

"Tell me what you mean now." vs. "Tell me what you mean, now!"

The initial *now* followed by a comma in a sentence ending with a question mark functions as a kind of mollifying element in the sentence. It establishes the speaker's tone which seems thoughtful, implying a real effort to understand what the person addressed is getting at.

Without the comma, the tone of the sentence shifts. When you read "now what" without a pause, the stress falls naturally on the first word (*"now* what") and lends the sentence a tone of annoyance, exasperation, or impatience.

The second pair also shows how the comma determines tone. You can hear the whine where the comma is not used before *now*: "Golly gosh, you keep changing your mind, what is it you mean by that *this* time?" With *now* set off at the end, it functions almost as an expletive, such as "damn it!"

To further illustrate:

You know I love you.

————

You know, I love you.

Both of these are correct, but they mean different things. The first sentence has an implied subordinating element (*that*, as in "You know [that] I love you"), which transforms the clause "I love you" in its entirety into the object of the verb *know* (i.e., that I love you is what you know).

In the second sentence, "you know" can be read as an interjection, such as *look* or *gee* or *listen*. It can also be seen as a kind of emphatic declaration— "You *know* . . . " The point is that the comma creates two independent elements—either an interjection and an independent clause or two independent clauses—not a single statement.

You ignore commas at your peril! They seriously affect how any sentence is read. Consider this: What if, instead of "Call me Ishmael," Melville had written, "Call me, Ishmael"?

What would *Moby Dick*'s second sentence have been? "Sure, dude. When's a good time to catch you?"

INTERNAL PUNCTUATION: OTHER MARKS

Beyond the comma, there is a family of other punctuation marks that we use within sentences. These punctuation marks include **semicolons** (;), **ellipses**

(. . .), and **parentheses**, and you should take some care with them—even if you think you know how to use them. Unlike our critical or journalistic confreres, we creative types can experiment with punctuation just as we do with language or form—and we enjoy doing it. Some creative writers tend to think employing the unexpected colon or apostrophe makes a piece of writing look sophisticated, but, too often, this merely makes the writing look strange or pretentious. Get to know how these marks are used conventionally. Then, when you choose to break the established rules, you at least will be making an informed choice.

Semicolons

The **semicolon** has enjoyed recently a peculiar and entirely unmerited popularity. Some writers sprinkle semicolons throughout their texts with great profligacy, each mark placed as if it just seemed "time" to put one in. The fact is, while the semicolon is extremely valuable, its correct usage is limited.

Despite a name that appears to relate it to the colon, it makes better sense to think of the semicolon as the combination of the two elements that constitute it—a period and a comma. (Imagine it as a fraction with the comma as the denominator and the period as the numerator.) It functions as a kind of half-period, but because its dominant element is the comma, it cannot be used as a terminal mark of punctuation. It is generally used in one of two instances: linking independent clauses and separating items in lists.

LINKING INDEPENDENT CLAUSES

The first of these is to link independent clauses; that is, those clauses that could stand as discrete sentences or be linked with a coordinating conjunction (*and, but, while,* and so on).

Deborah spent a long time at the fair; she rode every ride at least twice.

This sentence can be rewritten as

Deborah spent a long time at the fair. She rode every ride at least twice.

or:

Deborah spent a long time at the fair, and she rode every ride at least twice.

When you use a comma to avoid repeating a verb, separate the independent clauses of the sentence with a semicolon.

Some people seemed friendly; others, a bit wary.

That sentence is a "contraction" of the following:

Some people seemed friendly. Others seemed a bit wary.

In a sentence where the second (or third, and so on) independent clause is introduced by such conjunctive adverbs as *however, consequently, therefore, thus, besides,* or *then,* without a coordinating conjunction a semicolon is used to separate the clauses.

Marsha insisted on going to the monastery; thus, she learned the difficult truth.

If a coordinating conjunction appears, the sentence is punctuated as follows:

Marsha insisted on going to the monastery, and, thus, she learned the difficult truth.

Of course, this can also be written as two sentences.

Marsha insisted on going to the monastery. Thus, she learned the difficult truth.

Some argue that using a semicolon is better than either writing separate sentences or linking two clauses with a coordinating conjunction when the second clause expresses the consequence of the first one.

Milton loved merely being around Vivian; her beauty intoxicated him.

I'm not entirely convinced that the foregoing is more effective than the next two examples.

Milton loved merely being around Vivian, for her beauty intoxicated him.

———

Milton loved merely being around Vivian. Her beauty intoxicated him.

In complicated clauses that contain commas and coordinating conjunctions, a semicolon at the end of the first clause can be a useful sign to the reader that she's about to encounter a different clause. Even in those instances, however, I'm inclined to depend on commas, syntax, and even division into two sentences rather than tossing in a semicolon.

Constance, Eunice, and Phillipa, Sandra's aunts, arrived, cold and tired, not on the 4:15 but the 6:19, and they soon made total nuisances of themselves.

Despite the fact that the first independent clause in the above sentence has six commas and three coordinating conjunctions, the sentence seems to read fine the way it is. If bothered by it, a writer could legitimately insert a semicolon after "6:19," though, frankly, why not then merely divide the sentence into two?

That might be the best alternative. Indeed, this particular example, while useful, is a bit over-the-top. It could benefit from repunctuation—for example, using dashes rather than commas to frame "cold and tired." Were there a comma in the second clause, the two clauses would *have* to be separated with a semicolon or into two sentences.

SEPARATING ITEMS IN LISTS

The other case where the semicolon is commonly employed is in "listings" of items including at least one item that contains a comma. Using commas to separate such elements could cause confusion for the reader.

Among the people who were invited to the reception were Arnold

Schmaltz, the senator from Tennessee; Candida DiGiorgio, who had recently published her *Critique of American Morals*; and Loren Gillison, editor of the *Daily Blat*, noted webmaster, and famous wit.

Common examples of items that contain a comma are a city and state (or country or county) and a date presented in full with its month, day, and year in that order.

Anita's trip took her to Paris, France; Berlin, Germany; and Warsaw, Poland.

Timothy wrote letters of complaint to American Tourister on April 24, 1998; October 3, 1998; and January 4, 1999.

However, in a list of dates arranged with the day preceding the month, commas are used in that each individual date requires no punctuation.

Timothy wrote letters of complaint to American Tourister on 24 April 1998, 3 October 1998, and 4 January 1999.

There are other instances in which a semicolon is appropriate. Writers sometimes employ them to avoid the choppiness that can result from too many sequential short sentences. Even then, however, it may make more sense to rework a paragraph and rephrase its sentences rather than depending on semicolons to link things together.

I won't deny that some publications—both *The New York Times* and *The New Yorker* come to mind—manifest a real addiction to the semicolon. It has become the laudanum of punctuation marks. (I employ the images of drug dependency intentionally here—and if you don't know what laudanum is, look it up.)

Ellipses

As with the semicolon, many writers have grown enamored of the **ellipsis**. This useful mark of punctuation has a relatively limited repertoire, though it has a great many more roles in creative work than in other contexts. In fiction or the personal essay, there is considerable subtlety in usage and form.

HOW TO MAKE AN ELLIPSIS

We all know an ellipsis is three dots. (Actually, it's sometimes four dots, but we'll get to that later. To render the dots in compliance with the consensus, use the period key for the dots, include an equal amount of space between each dot, and include a space between the ellipsis and the word preceding it.

> As Lincoln stated: "Four score and seven years ago our fathers brought forth . . . a new nation, conceived in liberty, and dedicated to the proposition that all men are created equal."

OMISSIONS

In journalism and critical writing, the ellipsis is employed to indicate material "missing" from a quotation from a cited source (i.e., material that is not being presented in the quotation). You can see in the foregoing example how the ellipsis shows that the words *upon this continent* have been deleted from the opening of the Gettysburg Address.

Some manuals of style (e.g., that of the Modern Language Association) direct writers to frame ellipses like those in our example with brackets—[. . .]—in order to emphasize that the present author is deleting material from the original text. This isn't just being fussy. After all, since a writer may quote from, say, *Gravity's Rainbow*, in which Thomas Pynchon himself employs ellipses, the reader needs a way to distinguish between ellipses that are the source's own and those that the writer is employing to indicate omissions.

Now, things begin to get a shade more complicated. Were you to arrest a quotation in midsentence, the ellipsis would appear *along with* the mark of terminal punctuation for the sentence as a whole, be it a period, a question mark, or an exclamation point. There is no space between the last word and the first period.

> Lincoln began: "Fourscore and seven years ago. . . . "

———

> Watching Nellie there in the game was painful. She was like Richard the Third at Bosworth Field—"A horse! A horse! My kingdom . . . !" I felt dismal.

THE UNFINISHED SENTENCE

In creative work, the ellipsis is used *in dialogue* to indicate that a sentence has simply dissolved into nothing.

> "I just don't understand how . . . " Mavis lowered her head and began to cry.

Note that three dots rather than four are employed. The spoken sentence is not, in fact, complete, so it has no terminal punctuation.

Similarly, the ellipsis is employed when somebody begins a sentence, fails to finish it, begins another, and so on, as in moments of confusion or when "coming to" after unconsciousness. This is not the same as stammering, which is usually indicated with a hyphen, as will be illustrated later.

> "What the . . . ! But, Andrea, how could you think . . . ? Darling, tell me it just isn't . . . Please!"
> ———
> "Huh? Where am? . . . What happened to . . . Oh, my head!"

You can see how this is getting really subtle. The sentences above are unfinished, just like the one where Mavis started crying. However, some of them include a terminal punctuation mark. When an unfinished sentence is a question or an exclamation, the appropriate punctuation mark should be included for the reader's benefit.

PAUSES

The ellipsis can also indicate a pause, though it's easy to get carried away with this. Most always, the best way to signal a pause is the simple full stop of a period. Too, pauses are often implicit in the speaker's words. The ellipsis, though useful, can seem merely intrusive, a kind of overkill. Finally, pauses may be more forcefully indicated by interrupting the quotation with a gesture, an expression, or a phrase such as—gee, I don't know—"she paused"?

The ellipsis performing this function seems more appropriate in a script or screenplay than in a narrative text. These theatrical works may be the source of this punctuation mark's increasing popularity in creative prose. In those other genres, the ellipsis is quite important, given that the writers try to keep use of narrative to a minimum. But novelists and essayists do not operate under the same restrictions.

In the following, I'd argue that the second, third, and fourth versions are more effective than the first, which also might be written, "Are you ready? Are you?"

> "Are you ready? . . . Are you?"
> ———
> "Are you ready? Are you!"
> ———
> "Are you ready? Well, are you?"
> ———
> "Are you ready?" Ellen frowned and tossed her head. "Are you?"

The last three sentences indicate in different ways the pause signaled by the ellipsis in the first. In the second, the reader may realize there's been a beat between the two sentences only ex post facto upon hitting that impatient exclamation point. In the third and forth examples, the *well* and the interpolated narrative literally provide the pauses in the language itself.

In sum, it is not "wrong" to use the ellipsis in this fashion, but it is frequently unnecessary.

INTERRUPTIONS

Some editors endorse the use of ellipses to indicate an interruption. I'm inclined to use a dash instead to prevent confusion as to whether the speaker is interrupted or simply leaving his utterance unfinished, as we discussed earlier. Consider the following:

> "If only I had . . . "
> "Thought about it, you wouldn't have done it."

The intent here is to script an interruption, but, as it stands, you could also read this as the first speaker allowing his words to drift off to nothing and the second speaker, upon realizing this, completing the unfinished sentence.

You might argue that using the four-dot ellipsis ("If only I had. . . . ") would resolve any confusion, as it would indicate that the first speaker intended to finish his sentence, but was interrupted. But this asks the reader to distinguish between a three-dot and a four-dot ellipsis in order to correctly interpret the passage. Even if both utterances included an ellipsis, it would not be entirely clear if we were dealing with an interruption or a pause on the part of both speakers.

Hey, make it easy on yourself. Use a dash.

"If only I had—"
"Thought about it, you wouldn't have done it."

OVERHEARD CONVERSATIONS

Another place the ellipsis crops up in creative work is in the part of a conversation that a third party overhears. This is most common where one character hears another character talking on the telephone.

As Sandra made her sandwich, Barcley picked up the phone.
"Oh, hi, Marty. . . . So, how did the test go? . . . You aced it? . . . "

There are complications inherent in this as well, however. This topic is addressed at length in chapter ten, "Setting Dialogue and Thoughts."

Parentheses

With **parentheses**, remember the meaning of *parenthetically*. Parenthetical material is secondary, not essential to the understanding of a particular topic. When you skim a scholarly article, something you see between parentheses is, theoretically, something you don't even have to read.

The date borne by the American Declaration of Independence (July 4, 1776) has achieved almost universal resonance.

Given this, be cautious. You don't want your audience to think that what is between parentenses is, in fact, parenthetical. Still, this mark of punctuation has peculiar uses in fiction and other creative work.

ASIDES

In creative prose, parentheses are sometimes employed as a means of setting apart stray thoughts or asides.

Maybe I could hide out for a couple weeks (yeah, right!), or I'd find out I'd won the Publisher's Clearing House Sweepstakes and could buy a ticket on a slow boat to China (fat chance!).

———

She noted Paula's dress (fuchsia), shoes (clunky), and makeup (thick). What on earth did Maury see in her?

Likewise, use parentheses to include another punctuation mark—usually a question mark or exclamation point—in the body of a sentence in order to express doubt, surprise, or the like.

So, what was I to make of all this? Brenda actually wanted (!) to meet Randy. She thought his stunt at the office party was cute (?), and she had told Maryanne he had a lovely smile.

Note, however, that the same effect could be achieved in other ways.

So, what was I to make of all this? Brenda actually *wanted* to meet Randy. She thought his stunt at the office party was "cute," and she had told Maryanne he had a lovely smile.

In general, unless you can come up with a good reason to employ parentheses, don't do it. For many apprentice writers, parentheses become a kind of crutch, allowing for the quick insertion of information that would be better presented in a more leisurely and traditional fashion. Too, it can become the means of introducing some cheap irony into a piece, that "wink, wink, nudge, nudge" we've become all too accustomed to.

Charlie entered, all three hundred pounds of him (What a stud!).

The world has surely had enough of this kind of thing over the last decade.

Brackets and Braces

Two other internal "vertical" marks of punctuation that are far rarer even than parentheses in creative prose are **brackets** ([ ]) and **braces** ({ }). Authors sometimes use them eccentrically instead of parentheses or italics, but this usually looks odd or, worse, amateurish.

About the only way these might come up in a story or memoir is, in the case of brackets, when the writer quotes some other document in which they would logically appear.

> On the bus, Berthina scanned her brother's letter.
>
> " . . . and Uncle Ralph told me 'I ain't [*sic!*] seen him.' I get so tired of being related to such a bunch of hicks!"
>
> She harumphed. College, she thought, was going to Davon's head in a big way.
>
> ———
>
> Rafe couldn't believe this happy accident. He pulled the crumpled ATM slip from his shirt pocket and, surreptitiously as he could, jotted down: "1st edition (Bailey's [1946? or '47 British?]) stolen from collection in 1953."

In both these instances, the brackets themselves appear in the text in question—the condescending letter from Berthina's brother or in Rafe's jotted note on the ATM slip.

The same idea holds true for braces.

> The table was exacting work, but it was such a perfect present for her grandmother. Painstakingly, Tabitha copied the information onto the shiny sheet of parchment:

Willa
Agnes
Flora   }   Aunt Sadie's schoolmates
Dorothy
Laura

These are peculiar marks of punctuation in creative prose. Striving to be unique or experimental, we may be tempted to use them. Remember, though, they draw attention to themselves, which is exactly what you, as author, generally *don't* want to have happen as you try to draw somebody into the world you create on the page.

Colons

The **colon**, like brackets and braces, is more likely to appear in critical writing than in creative work. It has a somewhat formal and fussy reputation. That may be unfair, but that's the way it is. The storyteller most commonly uses it to signal real emphasis when introducing a list of things or to emphasize an elaboration of what has already been stated.

> For the gang members, the rules of the game were simple: accept the *capo*'s orders unquestioningly, perform the rubout, and never get caught.

> Barry entered into any situation with the same attitude: never apologize.

From time to time in fiction, writers use a colon to introduce a quotation into the narrative in order to make it especially emphatic.

> Each time she glanced at her overnight bag, Amanda remembered Tyrone's words vividly: "Get out and never come back!"

Dashes

The **dash** is the colon's cooler, more laid-back cousin. Perhaps because it is horizontal rather than vertical, it seems to be "faster" than the colon. We read through a dash more quickly than we do a colon, which is closer to the full stop of a period.

As you will see, the dash may also be faster in the racier and more colloquial sense. It's something of a gigolo, popping up—to coin a phrase—in place of all sorts of other marks, functioning as both internal and, on very specific occasions, terminal punctuation. This is well and good, but be careful. The dash can connote a particular reading of a sentence in ways a period or a colon, for example, does not. Too, because the dash is punctuation's original good-time guy, it is frequently overused, appearing promiscuously all over the text. In a diary entry or a letter to a friend or a hurried note, this is fine, but beware of sprinkling dashes too frequently in more formal and controlled prose.

SUBSTITUTION OF THE DASH FOR THE COLON

You could use a dash instead of a colon in any of the preceding examples, as shown here.

For the gang members, the rules of the game were simple—accept the *capo*'s orders unquestioningly, perform the rubout, and never get caught.

———

Barry entered into any situation with the same attitude—never apologize.

———

Each time she glanced at her overnight bag, Amanda remembered Tyrone's words vividly—"Get out and never come back!"

In these renditions, I think you'll agree that the sentences read more quickly. At a colon, you pause, then read the phrase that follows. The dash leads you into the phrase that follows. It is like a traffic arrow pointing you onward, as opposed to the colon's yellow light. The colon says: "Slow down." The dash says—"Floor it."

DASHES AND LISTS

Dashes are used to set off midsentence lists that contain commas and, hence, might prove confusing if framed with more commas. In the following example, parentheses could also be employed, but these would make MacArthur's phrase seem less significant, more parenthetical, than you may want.

Douglas MacArthur's characterization of military service—duty, honor, country—is perhaps the most famous such definition in American history.

INTERRUPTIONS

As we noted when discussing the ellipsis, in dialogue, the dash is employed to indicate interruption, by either another speaker or some sudden or violent shift in the action.

"I just don't want to—"

"Oh, shut up!"

———

"Just keep your eyes on the road and you'll be—"
Crash!

Compare the last example to one used when we talked about exclamation points.

The fuse was quickly consumed, and then . . . Ka-boom!

With the ellipsis, there is an implicit pause between the instant when the fuse was completely consumed and the explosion. Now read

The fuse was quickly consumed, and then—Ka-boom!

Here, we hear that "Ka-boom" immediately.

All this is discussed further in chapter ten, "Setting Dialogue and Thoughts."

One last note: Some word processing programs include a function to insert a dash. You can also produce the dash by hitting the hyphen key twice rather than once.

Hyphens

While we're on the subject, we might as well talk about the **hyphen**. It is used less than it once was in typed texts, because, these days, people generally work on computers. Most software automatically adjusts spacing so as to avoid breaking a word at the end of a line.

Paul thought that poor, silly, lonely Stephen was too inclined to anthro-pomorphize his pets.

You might want to use a hyphen for this purpose in a sentence that includes some kind of complicated adjective employing slashes or hyphens and causing a line of text that is only ten words long.

So they bumped over the bad road, Ruth and this

Portuguese/Spanish/Italian/French/English prince she had come to know.

You can see how the computer, confused by those slashes, sends that roll call of nationalities onto the same line. It would look better, though, as follows:

So they bumped over the bad road, Ruth and this Portuguese/Spanish/Italian/French/English prince she had come to know.

COMPOUND WORDS

Hyphens commonly appear in some **compound words**, in order to help prevent confusion. Remember that compounds can be rendered as two words ("skin game"), as hyphenated words ("skin-deep"), or as a single word ("skintight"). Your best guide to choosing a form is your dictionary. Most provide a list of words that are conventionally hyphenated. Take a look under *well* for an example—or for abundant examples.

Generally, if a compound term does not appear in the dictionary, it should be written as two separate words. Remember, I said "generally."

When **a compound adjective precedes a noun** and begins with what, in context, is actually an adverb (*better, lower, least*, for example) modifying the other part of the compound and not the noun, it is often hyphenated to prevent confusion. Compare the following:

the best priced item

_____

the best, priced item

_____

the best-priced item

The first example is ambiguous. We can't really tell if *best* modifies *priced* or *item*. In the second, *best* clearly modifes *item*, so this is the best item that bears a price. In the third example, the hyphen makes it apparent that the item that is available for the best price.

Note that when **the adjective falls after a verb** rather than preceding the noun it modifies, the compound adjective is generally *not* hyphenated.

The item Kelly chose was the best priced.

But

Kelly chose the best-priced item.

When the **first part of the compound is evidently an adverb** (e.g., it ends in *ly* or is a common adverb such as *very* or *much*), the hyphen usually is *not* necessary.

The fully matured Monet painted furiously.

———

The very serious student will read the text in greater depth.

OTHER COMPOUND ADJECTIVES

Hyphenate a compound adjective when it includes a participial form (*-ing* or *-ed*) and precedes the noun it modifies.

The roast chicken provided a lip-smacking good time!

———

Marsh confronted the hate-filled deacon.

———

At the agreed-upon hour, the two met in secret.

———

It was a hideous, rat-infested basement.

Do the same with **compound adjectives composed of a number and a noun** when they precede the noun modified.

four-door sedan

———

Mary's fifteenth-floor apartment

———

early-eighteenth-century poetry

Hyphenate **a compound adjective when, without the hyphen, the expression might be confusing.**

Jewish-history students should now report to the monitor.

At best, context would make it apparent that this is about students of Jewish history rather than history students who were Jewish, but the hyphen makes this absolutely clear.

COEQUAL NOUNS

Use a hyphen to separate **coequal nouns**, which indicate that somebody wears two hats, for example:

> lawyer-homemaker
>
> ———
>
> farmer-orator
>
> ———
>
> secretary-treasurer

Do *not* use a hyphen when one noun modifies the other, for example:

> brother love
>
> ———
>
> mother figure
>
> ———
>
> city manager

ONOMATOPOEIC WORDS

Onomatopoeic words, which try to imitate a sound literally, are usually hyphenated if composed of more than one element.

> clickety-clack
>
> ———
>
> tick-tock
>
> ———
>
> hee-hee

PHRASAL ADJECTIVES

Use hyphens to separate the elements of **phrasal modifiers** when used as adjectives.

Lonnie was one of those beer-and-pepperoni-pizza dudes.

———

Mortimer gave her an oh-my-god-I-can't-believe-you-just-said-that glare.

STAMMERING

In creative prose, when portraying a **stammer** or **stutter**, use hyphens.

"Wh-wh-what do you me-me-mean."

———

"D-d-d-did you?"

PREFIXES

On the whole, you do *not* use hyphens to separate **standard prefixes** (*anti, un, ex, non,* etc.) from the nouns to which they are affixed, but this can vary. If the noun is capitalized or if a resulting term would be difficult to pronounce or ambiguous, do employ a hyphen. No hyphen is used in these words:

antidemocratic

———

unaffordable

But

de-emphasize

———

re-mark (meaning "to put another mark on something," not "to make a comment").

NUMBERS

Numbers between twenty and one hundred are hyphenated when they stand alone or as elements of larger numbers.

twenty-nine

———

three hundred thirty-three

———

one thousand four hundred sixty-six

Of course, numbers and how they are rendered are a whole issue in themselves, as discussed on page 152.

OVERSTRIKE

The hyphen is used to produce an **overstrike**—the "lining through" of a word or phrase in print. This usage is now rare in that most software includes an overstrike feature that achieves this effect without actually striking out anything. In creative work, there might be a couple of cases where you would employ this. One such instance is the reproduction of text written by one of your characters.

> She looked with horror at the note taped to the refrigerator.
> "How could you have taken my ~~damned~~ stash. I thought you were a Christian, and now I find out you've been ~~stealing~~ ripping off my stuff ever since you got here!"

WORDS ENDING IN A HYPHEN

Very rarely, a word appears with a hyphen **affixed at the end**. The classic instance of this is in reference to a former spouse as "my ex-," though "ex" with no hyphen now appears in the dictionary.

* * *

As you can see, the hyphen is a busy guy in the world of punctuation and can be, according to house style, variously employed. Depending on whom you read or write for, it can be "right" to write "Post-Modern," "post-modern," "Postmodern," and so on. If you are tempted to hyphenate a word or expression, do so. It indicates to an editor that you are aware that this mark is used as a means of fusing words that haven't merged into one.

If she takes it out, let her—unless taking it out changes the meaning.

Apostrophes

The **apostrophe** (') does duty in English in a number of ways. Chapter ten shows how it is used as a single quotation mark. Most commonly, it's employed in two ways: One we've already discussed, and the other is shown twice in this sentence.

POSSESSIVES

An apostrophe along with the letter *s* indicates **possession**, as in "Mary's purse," "Ben's house," "the officers' badges." For the kinds of problems that can arise with this, see chapter eight, "Plurals and Possessives."

CONTRACTIONS

Apostrophes are also used for **contractions** in English. In creative work, both in dialogue and in certain kinds of narrative, contractions are much more common and appropriate than they are when you're writing a study about mitochondria in basal cells of the spine or about Mithraism among members of the Vth Roman Legion.

Contractions indicate how words are pronounced when they are subjected to "eliding"—leaving out a letter or sound as we speak. Hence, we write "didn't" for "did not," "he's" for "he is," even "Mike'd've" for "Mike would [or could] have." In a contraction, an apostrophe takes the place of the letter or letters that are not pronounced. It does not replace the space that existed between the full words (for "had not," we write "hadn't," *not* "had'nt").

A common apostrophe error is the confusion of the words *its* and *it's*. It might seem logical that *it's* is the possessive form of *it*, but it is (or it's) not. Simply remember that no possessive pronoun uses an apostrophe. You would never write "That book is her's."

Similarly *whose*, a possessive, and *who's*, the contraction of *who is*.

Who's to say whose house looks better?

Another common error occurs with contractions with the auxiliary verb *have*, which many writers hear not as "-'ve," but as the preposition *of*. "We could have" is correctly written in its contracted form as "We could've," *not* as "We could of." Check out the earlier example. "Mike'd've," not "Mike'd of," is the proper rendition of either "Mike could have" or "Mike would have."

In the same way, we write "I'd've" rather than "I'da" for "I would have," and other examples abound.

DIALECT

For fiction, writers often employ the apostrophe to indicate other forms of eliding. The most common of these is to indicate the dropped *g* at the end of present participles and gerunds, those "-ing" words. Present participles are employed as part of the progressive tense ("I was sleeping when she called") or as adjectives ("Roscoe was a star running back"). Gerunds are "-ing" words employed as nouns ("Sleeping is his favorite thing in the whole wide world").

Authors often use this tactic in dialogue in order to capture the sound of how a particular character speaks. To render such a word, the writer replaces the final *g* with an apostrophe.

"I was sleepin' when she called."

———

"Sleepin' is his favorite thing in the whole wide world."

This is fine, and it's very common. Remember, though, that a speaker who drops a *g* in one instance probably does so consistently, so every time he speaks a present participle or gerund, the writer has to use an apostrophe to replace the *g*. Trying to capture these kinds of peculiarities of speech can make things muddy. A certain speaker, for example, might tend to elide parts of the entire phrase "sleeping is his," which would then be written "sleepin's 'is."

To indicate how somebody talks, it is almost always easier to give a simple narrative detail and be done with it.

Art's recently acquired habit of always dropping the final *g* drove his college-educated parents crazy, something he knew all too well.

This kind of play with the spoken word is often used when to render various **dialects**. For further discussion of this issue, go to chapter fifteen.

ESOTERIC PUNCTUATION MARKS
Accent Marks

Accent marks are not native to English, but, because the language is always picking up strangers from other tongues, accent marks may appear in your prose. Creative writers have traveled more and had greater contact with other cultures and subcultures, both domestically and overseas, than at any other time in our history, and this often manifests itself in the writers' stories. Further, a larger number of authors these days are products of bilingual families or neighborhoods. It's worth it, then, to talk about accent marks in our discussion of punctuation.

COMMON ACCENT MARKS

Accent marks serve a variety of functions in different languages. In some, an accent indicates which syllable in a word is stressed; in others, an accent signals the particular way of pronouncing a vowel or consonant. For example, in Spanish, words ending in vowels or in an *n* or an *s* are stressed on the penultimate (next to last) syllable; words ending in all other consonants are stressed on the final syllable. The **acute accent** (´) is used to show an exception to this rule or, in certain instances, to show that a word (such as *what* or *which*) is being used interrogatively.

"*Olé!*" they screamed as the matador sidestepped the charging bull.

———

"*¿Qué decías?*" ["What were you saying?"]

In French, the acute accent affects the pronunciation of a vowel. In a word such as *élan*, the acute accent tells us that the *e* has the sound of the English long *a*, not that the *e* is stressed. Another example is *coup d'état*, which is pronounced "coo day-TAH," not "coo DAY-tah."

The acute accent is the one you're most likely to come across, though others that occur in other languages crop up from time to time in words that English has borrowed.

The **grave accent** (`) appears in a number of French words we have merrily toted across the English Channel and then across the Atlantic; a few of these words are *crèche*, *mise-en-scène*, and *à la carte*. Once again, this accent indicates how the marked vowel is pronounced, not which syllable is stressed.

It is also used in English to indicate the outright pronunciation of a syllable that is usually unstressed. This is more common in poetry than prose, and it is intended mostly these days to sound archaic or overdramatic.

"But Agnes," Pete cried, "you are my belovèd."

The **cedilla** (¸) appears in words borrowed from French and Portuguese, and it indicates that a *c* carries an "s" sound rather than a "k" sound. Some examples are *soupçon, curaçao,* and *façade.*

The **circumflex** (^), another French import, is that little caret that appears over a vowel in certain words or expressions and, again, affects the pronunciation of the vowel. It often indicates some form of contraction that has become conventional. This is illustrated by words such as *coup de grâce, papier-mâché,* and *table d'hôte.*

The **tilde** (˜), a squiggly line above a letter, again is a pronunciation guide. In Portuguese, it indicates nasalization resulting in a sound similar to the English combination "ng." In Spanish, the tilde means that an *n* is pronounced "ny," as is obvious in our rendering of the Spanish word *cañon* as *canyon.*

The **dieresis** (in Latin-based languages) or **umlaut** (in Germanic ones) are both formed the same way—two dots over a vowel (¨)—though they function differently. In English and French, the dieresis indicates that two vowels are pronounced separately rather than being melded together. It used to be quite common in English, appearing in such words as *coördinate* and *reënact,* which we now spell with no punctuation at all. It still pops up in a handful of words, usually French in origin (*naïf,* for example, or *noël*), though even this is changing.

In German, a vowel marked with an umlaut is pronounced differently than the same vowel without an umlaut. This mark indicates a melding of vowel sounds. An illustration you are probably familiar with is the spelling of the name of Hitler's air marshall, Hermann Göring. A word with an umlauted vowel can also be spelled with an *e* following what would have been the umlauted vowel: "Hermann Göring" becomes "Herman Goering."

DISTINGUISHING HOMOGRAPHS

We sometimes use accent marks to distinguish identically spelled words that have different pronunciations, grammatical functions, or connotations. These are referred to as "homographs." An example of this are the two forms (one unaccented, the other accented) of *expose.*

Yvonne would expose Bob for the fraud he was.

———

Her exposé of Bob's activities caused tremendous scandal.

This appears to be the same word. The accent distinguishes the pronunciations and helps differentiate the verb from the noun.

Further, accents can emphasize the distinction between a word that has a "domesticated" English usage but is still sometimes employed in accord with its definition in its original language. A classic case of this is *café*, which in a number of Romance languages means "coffee" and, by extension, "a place where coffee and light meals are served." In the latter sense, the word has become Anglicized and is usually (but not always) written without an accent. Note the following noir example.

> We met at a greasy little cafe off Hudson Street on Fourteenth. When she ordered a caffe latte, I knew she was entirely out of her depth.
> "Where do you think you are," I sneered, "the Café des Artistes?"

THE VANISHING ACCENT MARK

Often, the inclusion of an accent mark on a word borrowed from another language is inversely proportional to the frequency of that word's use in the common parlance. However, as in the case of *expose/exposé*, accents can have a real usefulness in helping English speakers distinguish two homographs. For the most part, accents simply vanish as particular words become more common in English. We hardly think of *brassiere* or *premiere*—accented in French—as foreign words at all. We spell the city of San Jose without an accent on the final *e*, and we turned the Spanish word meaning "mountain"—*montaña*—into the name of a state.

Other Rarely Used Punctuation Marks

Other marks and symbols on your keyboard should be considered, at least briefly, because you might have occasion to employ them in a creative text. These are the **underline** (_), the **ampersand** (&), the **asterisk** (*), the **slash** (or **bar** or **virgule**—(/), the **"each"** or **"at"** symbol (@) and the **backslash** (\).

UNDERLINE

The **underline** (or **underscore**) was once commonly used in manuscripts to let the printer know that he should set a word or passage in *italics*. In this digital age, where we shift fonts at will, this is rarer, though some publishers still prefer that italicized passages appear in underlined roman type. Underlining can also be used in cases where you are reproducing a handwritten text.

> Dora's letter certainly demonstrated how she loved to play the victim.
> "How could you even <u>think</u> that I would have told Marvin! He's your
> <u>boyfriend</u>, for God's sake. I wouldn't so much as <u>imply</u> to him you'd
> even <u>seen</u> Mark again, much less <u>slept</u> with him!"

You might use the underline to add emphasis in a passage that is already italicized.

> His thoughts swirled through his head in a jumble: *Murray <u>isn't</u> dead!*
> *He's living in <u>Queens</u>, just four subway stops away! How had he managed*
> *to just—what?—<u>vanish</u> for twenty years?*

AMPERSAND

The only appropriate literary uses of the **ampersand** are in a reproduced handwritten text or in an instance where it is actually employed, such as in the name of a company. American Telephone and Telegraph is, after all, now officially AT&T. Here are some examples.

> "I'm really looking forward to seeing you & the folks over Christmas,"
> he wrote.

——

> There before him was the flickering neon sign: "Mulvaney & Sons
> Plumbing, Your Pipes Never Had It So Good!".

ASTERISK

The **asterisk** is the most common of what printers refer to as "dingbats," "wingdings," or, more elegantly, "vignettes." These symbols also include ☞, ✉, ❀, ☛, and the ever popular ☙.

The asterisk appears in creative texts when a white space indicating a transition falls at the top or the bottom of a page and, hence, is difficult for the reader to recognize. In these cases, center three asterisks on the last line of one page or the first line of the next page:

* * *

You sometimes see the asterisk replacing an ellipsis to indicate a deletion, though this is not standard. It also has shown up as an alternative to the period in abbreviations, most famously in *M*A*S*H*. It can replace a letter in a word, too. For example, Orthodox Jews are forbidden to write the word *God*, so they could replace the *o* with an asterisk: "G*d." In this case, however, a hyphen would do just as well ("G-d") and is much more common.

In some instances (Manuel Puig's *Kiss of the Spider Woman* comes to mind) the asterisk is used to direct the reader to a footnote. Obviously, this is dependent on your story and how you choose to tell it.

SLASH OR BAR OR VIRGULE

Some people substitute the **slash** or **bar** or **virgule** or **solidus** (nice word, huh?) for the hyphen, though this is nonstandard. It is sometimes appropriate when the use of a hyphen or conjunction might prove confusing or clumsy.

> Any man/boy or woman/girl is eligible for membership if all other criteria (residency and affirmation of faith) are met.

This avoids the constructions "man-boy" and "woman-girl" (are these some kind of synonyms for *teenager?*) or the clunkiness of "man or boy or woman or girl," though why not just write "Anyone, regardless of gender or age, . . . "?

The slash also is employed in some instances of absolute equivalencies, most notably in "and/or."

> Millicent indicated that the document would pass muster in court if signed by his mother and/or her legal representative.

The slash can also appear in the rendering of numbers—e.g., fractions (9/16, 24/37)—or dates, as shown here:

Born 7/29/43   Died 11/9/88

Slashes are also used when poetry is quoted in a piece of prose without being set off separately. Slashes indicate where line breaks fall.

> There in the Vermont darkness, as the snow gently grazed her cheek, she could not help but whisper: "Whose woods these are I think I know/ His house is in the village though. . . . "

THE "AT" SYMBOL AND THE BACKSLASH

The **"each"** or **"at"** symbol (@) once showed up in a story only as part of a business document or a sign ("Strawberries: 4 boxes @ $8.95"). The **backslash** (\) didn't appear on most typewriter keyboards at all. Computers have changed all of this, of course. It would be impossible for us to use certain software, access some Web sites, or even send an e-mail without these two symbols.

Still, your use of these in creative work is likely to be limited, at least in the immediate future, to reproduction of those particular kinds of texts within a larger story.

> Painstakingly, he began to tap in code as Lorton had instructed: c:\delete . . .

———

> Who the hell was *flyingboat@qnet.com*?

OTHER SYMBOLS

Your keyboard has other symbols, some of which—the signs for dollar ($), percent (%), plus (+), equals (=), or number (#, also sometimes called the "pound" or the "hash" sign)—you might have occasion to use in appropriate contexts, such as

> She owed him $5,229.14 at 9.9% interest!

———

> Marylee + Malcolm's ring = Buddy's broken heart.

———

> There Babs was, contestant #311.

These symbols can be effective, but be careful. They can cloy quickly, and then you're reduced to merely being cute.

* * *

I hope you recognize just how significant your punctuation is. It determines how your prose reads, and it allows you to lend nuance to the words you write I heard a story about the scholar Peter Elbow, who used this sentence:

> He kissed her deeply and passionately.

Now, to demonstrate how punctuation influences our reading, consider the following variations. The exact meaning of each one differs because of how it is punctuated.

He kissed her, deeply and passionately.

———

He kissed her—deeply and passionately.

———

He kissed her. Deeply and passionately.

———

He kissed her. Deeply and passionately!

At best, you can use punctuation as a powerful tool in your own fiction and creative nonfiction.

10

Setting Dialogue and Thoughts

The English language has conventions regarding how dialogue should be set in print. For illustrations of these, look at virtually any volume of creative prose you have lying around the house. Writers do sometimes violate these norms (Toni Morrison and William Faulkner, to name but two), and the rules are not exactly the same as those for French or German or various other languages. Even in Great Britain, writers go about things somewhat differently. From publication to publication and publishing house to publishing house in the U.S., there are divergent schools of thought on how best to indicate, for example, an interruption. Nonetheless, this chapter sets forth what seem to be the general American conventions for rendering conversation on the page.

DIALOGUE

The first thing to remember when dealing with dialogue is that you should *not* depend on your knowledge of how to present in critical work quotations or citations from sources you are referencing. Setting speech in fiction or creative nonfiction is an entirely different exercise.

Standard Quotation

Standard quotation of source material in scholarly or journalistic work involves employing distinctive indentation and so on for longer passages, and the simple use of quotation marks for shorter ones. Various professional groups (the Modern Language Association, the American Psychological Association, historians, linguists, gangsters, and haberdashers, nowadays) all have their own notions of how best these citations should appear.

Fiction and memoirs normally include this kind of quotation only when the author reproduces some kind of text—a sign, a business card, a broadside pasted on a wall, a brochure a character is handed on the street, an academic paper or police report or some other document she happens to be reading—within the text of the story itself. For example:

Boris presented his card to Lydia with a considerable flourish, bowing slightly at the waist and clicking his heels.

She glanced at the beveled cardboard in her hand:

Boris Antonio García y Manfredo, Esq.
Sculptor

——

Rushing down Forty-third Street to make it to her dressing room on time, Renata saw the announcement posted on phone pole after phone pole with Edgar's review prominently displayed:

"Renata Shurock's performance is one that Katherine Hepburn—nay, Katherine Cornell!—might envy!"

Edgar Billingsgame
The Evening Cloudburst

——

Wendall turned the brittle pages of the diary where Alphonse had poured his heart out. Then, there it was:

In reading about it, what struck me was that choice he made, that poem he had learned on his own that those of my age all had to recite when we were schoolboys:

Dark is the night that covers me,
Black as a pit from pole to pole,
I thank whatever gods may be
for my unconquerable soul.

Rendering speech on the page is very different from these examples. Given that dialogue is so important in creative work, let's discuss in depth the various ways to deal with it.

Dialogue and Paragraphing

As you know, when you introduce a new subject, you start a new paragraph. The first line of a new paragraph is normally indented five spaces (the standard "default" for the first stroke of your tab key) from the left margin. Subsequent lines are flush with the left margin.

Lauren and Michael walked all the way to the bridge, through the deteriorating neighborhoods and then the shabby park along the riverside.

Michael wondered how beautiful the park had been a century ago.

In dialogue, each **new speaker** is a new subject, even if that speaker says nothing more than "Huh?" Therefore, a new speaker's dialogue is set in a new paragraph.

"Do you want to go to the market, Jamie?" Sarah asked.

"Huh?"

"Do you want to go to the market with me? I have to pick up some potatoes to go with the roast tonight."

"Oh. Okay."

Only the first line of a speaker's dialogue gets indented. If the remarks of the character extend beyond one line, the part that falls onto the following line or lines begins at the left margin, as shown in Sarah's second question and her statement in the above example. (See "Extended Utterance by a Single Speaker" for an exception to this indentation rule.)

STANDARD DIALOGUE WITH TERMINAL SPEECH MARKERS

When you use **speech markers** (which some refer to as **speaker tags** or **attribution tags**) such as "he said," "she replied," "Tom answered," the character's uttered words are framed in quotation marks and set off by a comma.

"Get your coat on, then," Sarah said.

―――

Morton replied thoughtfully, "If that's what you really think."

If there is no speech marker, the uttered words of a statement end with a period.

"Get your coat on, then."

———

"If that's what you really think."

If the speaker's words are interrogative, use a question mark rather than a comma or period at the conclusion of his words. Do not use a comma if a speech marker follows the question.

"Are you ready to go, Jamie?"

A command or exclamation is followed by an exclamation point.

"Let's go, Jamie!"

———

"My God, Jamie, aren't you ready yet!"

Question marks and exclamation points are normally marks of terminal punctuation, but if a speech marker follows a question or exclamation, the speech marker's first letter should be lowercase, unless the first word is a proper name. No comma is necessary.

"Are you ready to go, Jamie?" asked Sarah.

———

"My God, Jamie, aren't you ready yet!" yelled Sarah.

———

"My God, Jamie, aren't you ready yet!" Sarah yelled.

DIALOGUE WITH INTERPOLATED SPEECH MARKERS

If a speech marker is interpolated into what a character says, the punctuation varies.

"Get your coat," Sarah said, "because it's cold outside."

Sarah's statement is a single sentence interrupted by the speech marker, so commas set the tag apart. However, contrast the punctuation in this example.

> "Get your coat," Sarah said. "Incidentally, did you ever find that Magic Marker you lost at school last week?"

Here, the *said* is followed by a period because the next words Sarah utters constitute a separate sentence.

DIALOGUE INTERPOLATED INTO NARRATIVE

If a line of dialogue appears in the midst of a narrative passage midsentence, frame the dialogue in quotation marks and set it apart with dashes.

> Deep in thought and soapsuds, Margo hadn't even noticed the new hire beside her. She pulled one gloved hand from the sink—"I'm Margo," she mumbled to him—and then returned to the dishes.

When the quotation appears at the end of a sentence, framing the dialogue in quotation marks and setting it off with a comma suffices.

> Driving down the highway toward his parents' house for the first time in ages, he could hear his mother's voice, "Don't you even think of racing the train, David." Over and over, all the years he was in high school, whenever he went out the door—as if it would have occurred to him after what happened to Willie. His dad used to say, "She'll just never get over it, Son, ever." Certainly, David had no reason to doubt his father on that one.

NARRATIVE INTERPOLATED INTO DIALOGUE

Trouble can arise when a character's line of dialogue is followed by a long narrative interpolation and then more of that character's speech. These moments you have to play by ear. Where the intervening narrative remains entirely within the speaker—her thoughts, her perspective, her feelings—both the dialogue and the narrative should appear in a single paragraph, as shown in this example.

"It's been a long, long time, Elliot," she said softly. Far too long, she thought. Long enough for her to forget just how being near him moved her, made her tremble somewhere deep inside where nobody could see and only she could feel. "Are you going to be visiting long?"

If one of these shifts to another character or if the real focus of the narrative is upon somebody other than the speaker, I'm inclined to set the narrative in a paragraph apart from the quoted dialogue, even if that means having to include a second speech marker, as illustrated in this example.

"It's been a long, long time, Elliot," she said softly.

Far too long, she thought, as he looked at her with those liquid brown eyes. From his very expression, she could see that evaluating gaze she recalled from the time they were children, that sizing up he did of others, his totaling of strengths and weaknesses that would allow him to figure out how to get what he wanted. Even at nine, he had been a heartbreaker.

"Are you going to be visiting long?" she asked.

VARYING SPEECH MARKERS

As long as we're talking about speech markers: Don't get overly inventive! Admittedly, the most common one—*said*—can get pretty old in a text when used over and over. I read a story where *said* appeared eleven times in the space of a single page. Still, trying to find alternatives can lead you toward expressions that sound peculiar. Some examples I've recently come upon are

"Let's just go the movies," Anne uttered.

——

"My mother's at the store," Ron expressed.

——

"Your library book is on the table," Mark declared.

——

"Constance took the subway, I think," Pat stated.

——

"But what if I didn't . . . , " Greta trailed.

The first two examples are simply awkward. *Utter* and *express* beg for objects.

These sentences can be recast so that those speech markers sound more appropriate and natural, though this involves considerable rewriting.

> Anne uttered her final disappointment in a plaintive sigh. "Let's just go the movies."
>
> ———
>
> Ron expressed his loneliness succinctly. "My mother's at the store, like always."

The examples of Mark's and Pat's dialogue are errors of tone. *Declare* and *state* imply a kind of power and formality that doesn't jibe with the words that are being "declared" and "stated." The location of a library book or Constance's chosen mode of transport don't justify such weighty verbs, though these would be perfectly appropriate in other instances.

> "No daughter of mine will be seen in public with the likes of Dirk Ramon!" Mark declared.
>
> ———
>
> "Linda Shipley was nowhere near the scene of the robbery, and you know it," Pat stated.

The example of Greta's speech confuses the speaker herself with the quality of her utterance. Greta didn't "trail," but her voice "trailed off."

LIMITATIONS ON PARTICULAR SPEECH MARKERS

Certain speech markers can only be used in specific contexts. You can only "ask" questions—

> "What time are you leaving?" Laura asked.

—and can generally only "answer," "respond," or "reply" to a question.

> "Sometime around four," Esther replied.

You "counter" something that has already been said—

"You're way off base on that one," Billy snapped.

"You're the one who's off base!" Suzanne countered.

—while a "retort" is a particularly sharp response, especially if the words are being turned back on the original speaker.

"That was a really stupid thing for us to do," Mary said.

"That was a really stupid thing for you to do!" Sally retorted.

Likewise, you really should only "exclaim" something that is truly exclamatory.

"That was a really stupid thing to do!" Mary exclaimed.

Be certain that the verb of utterance is in accord with the actual utterance.

OTHER ALTERNATIVES TO SAID

Ernest Hemingway purportedly claimed, on the assumption that the quality of what is uttered ought to be inherent in the dialogue itself, that a writer should never have to use *any* word except *said* to indicate speech. This is an admirable notion, and one that spurs us to craft dialogue with the same care we employ elsewhere in our prose. Still, English has a rich vocabulary describing different volumes and tones and types of speech, so why not take advantage of that?

These words, of course, are only appropriate in certain contexts, so don't have somebody "singing" or "whining" or "affirming" unless that suits what he's saying. Some words (*declare, lie, recall, speculate, state, vow*) can be used depending on *what* is said; others (*bark, coo, mutter, warble*), depending on *how* something is said. A few such words (*begin, conclude, continue*) relate to *where* in an utterance the quoted words fall. Many are commonly employed in tandem with an adverb or some other element.

"Nice tie," Galen mentioned casually.

"Oh, indeedy," Aunt Ella prattled on, "just the thing he'd want, I'm sure."

Don't overuse these *said* alternates; you can end up with conversations that sound like a day at the asylum or a trip to the zoo! All in all, *said* is a useful, all-purpose verb when it comes to marking speech.

Using Punctuation to Make Distinctions in Speech

Note that the punctuation of dialogue is governed by not only grammatical rules but also by the meaning a writer is trying to convey. A writer can make, solely with the punctuation, fine distinctions in the tone and inflection of what the characters say. In the following, Bobby first "yelps" the words he speaks, and next lets out a yelp and *then* speaks.

Bobby yelped, "Ow! You're hurting me!"

———

Bobby yelped. "Ow! You're hurting me!"

UTTERANCE VS. EXPRESSION OR GESTURE

Be careful about confusing verbs of utterance with those of expression, description, or gesture—for example, *smiled, frowned, glared, grimaced, nodded.* With dialogue, verbs of expression are usually (though not absolutely always) followed by a period or other terminal punctuation rather than a comma.

Angie murmured, "What a silly boy you are." [utterance]

———

Angie smiled. "What a silly boy you are." [expression]

———

"Don't do that!" his mother snapped at him. [utterance]

———

"Don't do that!" His mother pointed at him. [gesture]

Order of Utterance

When only two speakers are in conversation and the writer has established the "order of utterance," further speech markers are unnecessary as long as the reader can easily determine how the back-and-forth proceeds.

"But what if," Lana said, pulling the car to the curb, "you didn't say anything about it at all?"

"What do you mean?" Betty squeaked.

"Who says your mom has to know?"

"But I tell her everything."

"Everything? Like how you ripped off those lipsticks?"

"Of course I didn't tell her that!"

"See," Lana concluded triumphantly. "You just have to keep your mouth shut and no one's the wiser!"

USING ACTION TO DELINEATE SPEAKERS

Speech is almost always accompanied by some kind of gesture or action, so it's possible to distinguish between speakers by what they're doing while they're talking. If, say, JoAnne and Tim are at a restaurant, the writer can frame their conversation without using *said* at all.

JoAnne sipped delicately from her wineglass. "Do you really think it was that difficult?"

"I couldn't believe it." Tim shook his head. "I couldn't even answer half of their questions."

"It does sound pretty awful."

"I felt like a complete dope!" He snapped a breadstick. "I'll never make partner at this rate."

This technique can be especially useful when more than two speakers are involved in a scene. Rather than constantly employing *said* or other verbs of utterance, let the physical action or the speakers' locations cue the reader as to who is saying what.

Bobby flipped the baseball in Mark's direction. "So, how are you gonna handle it?"

"Hell if I know." Mark had to lunge to make the catch. "Patti won't even talk to me."

"Will you two quit moping around, for Lord's sake!" On the grass, Andy rolled over on his back and squinted in the sun. "Are we playing ball this afternoon or aren't we?"

Notice in the two foregoing examples that, beyond preventing repetitive verbs of utterance, the interpolated narrative goes beyond cueing the reader as to who is speaking. Those snippets of action and gesture give the passages dimension. We hear what's being said, *and* we see the speaker saying it. Tim's snapped breadstick and Andy's squint into the sun help us envision these characters' despair or impatience in a way that a simple *said* (or *lamented* or *whined*) never would.

Stage Directions

Don't use "stage directions"—fragments, usually featuring present participles indicating action—for your characters. Write complete sentences.

> Barbara nodded. "Have a seat." Walking toward the kitchen. "I'll be right back."

This kind of thing is conventional in plays and screenplays but not in prose, which would be better served by the following:

> Barbara nodded. "Have a seat." She walked toward the kitchen. "I'll be right back."

Dialogue Doing Narrative Work

Be cautious about asking dialogue to do too much narrative work. Dialogue can move the action of a story along or provide essential information about characters or events; nonetheless, the writer must be sure that what a character says would logically come from that character.

Apprentice writing often includes the mistake of having a speaker provide information to a listener that the listener would already be aware of.

> "Your boyfriend Tommy's roommate, Al, is such a hunk," Geena sighed.
>
> ———
>
> "Go down the block to your gramma's house."

In these instances, whoever Tommy's girlfriend is would presumably already know that he is her boyfriend, just as the grandchild in question would know that his gramma's house is down the block. This information needs to be transmitted to the reader in a subtler and more realistic way, whether through more extended dialogue or through narrative.

Extended Utterance by a Single Speaker

A character may speak in more than one paragraph sometimes—when making an argument or narrating an anecdote, for example. If this is the case, the writer needs to indicate that the same character's remarks continue. To signal this, do *not* close the quotation marks at the end of the first paragraph, open the second paragraph with quotation marks (so the reader will know that the speaking continues), and enter the "close quotes" when the speaker is finally done.

> "I can't imagine what Amanda was thinking," Quentin said, shaking his head. "She's always been so responsible, and now this. It's just incredible!
>
> "Anyway, Sarah, do you and Jamie still need a ride to the store? If you do, I can be by your place around seven o'clock."
>
> She sighed. "Thanks, Quentin, but we went this morning."

Incomplete Utterances

As suggested in chapter nine, when you want to indicate that someone is abruptly interrupted, use a dash.

> "I just don't want to—"
> "Oh, shut up!"

Some writers feel this can be even more effectively transmitted by not only concluding the first utterance with a dash, but opening the interruption with one as well. (One dash or two is another of those house style issues.)

> "I just don't want to—"
> "—Oh, shut up!"

If, on the other hand, somebody just stops talking, if her words just drift away, use a three-period ellipsis:

> "I just don't want to . . . "

Telephone Conversations

Remember from the discussion of the ellipsis that it is employed in situations in which only one speaker in a dialogue is overheard by a third party. The most frequent instance of this in prose is when presenting half of an exchange on the telephone. The example we employed in chapter nine was as follows:

> As Sandra made her sandwich, Barclay picked up the phone.
> "Oh, hi, Marty. . . . So, how did the test go? . . . You aced it? . . . Hey, terrific! . . . You're kidding me. . . . "

The last word of each of Barclay's utterances is followed by no space, a terminal punctuation mark, and then a three-dot ellipsis, the latter indicating the pause that Barclay allows for Marty's response.

This can get complicated. What if, for example, the test Marty had hoped to ace went badly? What if a surprised Barclay keeps flailing around for the right thing to say to his friend and just can't quite get it right?

> As Sandra made her sandwich, Barclay picked up the phone.
> "Oh, hi, Marty. . . . So, how did the test go? . . . What? . . . I mean . . . Well . . . It's just you were . . . were so sure about it. . . . Don't worry! . . . It'll work out. . . . You know . . . I mean . . . Just be cool, okay? . . . "

The ellipsis use here gets confusing. When is Barclay listening to Marty's response, and when is Barclay taking a run at a sentence, rethinking it, and starting all over again? The writer can desperately juggle three- and four-dot ellipses, but can he really expect a reader to pay such close attention to the punctuation that she will notice which is which? Would we writers want her to? This is a story, after all. What she ought to be concentrating on is Barclay, Marty, and Sandra.

For a scene such as this, it is probably easiest to integrate narrative detail into the passage to clarify for the reader precisely what's going on during the exchange.

> As Sandra made her sandwich, Barclay picked up the phone.
> "Oh, hi, Marty. How did the test go? . . . What!"

Reaching for the mayonnaise, Sandra saw her boyfriend's face blanche.

"But . . . I mean . . . Well . . . It's just you were . . . were so sure about it," he stammered.

Barclay held the receiver away from his ear. From all the way across the room, Sandra could hear the tinny whine of Marty's voice, even if she couldn't make out the words. He sounded accelerated, despairing, hysterical.

Finally, Barclay managed to interrupt. "Don't worry! It'll work out—"

He shook his head as Marty took off again.

"You know . . . I mean . . . Just be cool, okay?"

Terminal Punctuation and Quotation Marks

Note that, in each of the examples in this chapter, the final mark of punctuation for the words spoken falls within the quotation marks. In dialogue, quotation marks indicate what is spoken aloud. That period or question mark—though not literally voiced, of course—is an integral part of what is being said, because it indicates how something is said. You can see how essential punctuation is in the following illustration:

"Sam's conduct is inexcusable."
"Inexcusable."

———

"Sam's conduct is inexcusable."
"Inexcusable?"

———

"Sam's conduct is inexcusable."
"Inexcusable!"

In the first version, the second speaker merely repeats the declaration of the first. In the second, he questions whether Sam's conduct was inexcusable or how or why it was inexcusable. In the third, he is emphatic in his response, though we do not know whether that exclamatory response signifies agreement or disagreement ("Yes, his conduct is inexcusable!" vs. "What on earth do you mean, inexcusable!").

Quotations Within Quotations

Sometimes, you'll want your characters to employ quotations within quotations to indicate what somebody else remarked. Since your character's speech is already enclosed between standard double quotation marks, a quotation *by* your character gets marked with single quotation marks, which are rendered with the apostrophe key on a keyboard.

"Mary told me that Ed 'wasn't worth shooting,' and that was that."

If the sentence ends with the quotation within the quotation, close both sets of quotation marks, even though it looks funny.

"Mary told me that Ed 'wasn't worth shooting.' "

When what the speaker quotes and what she utters require different terminal punctuation, the appropriate mark appears for each.

"Patty, for Rex it's always the old 'Who's on first?' question."

"I know. I get so tired of his 'I'm the King of the World!' thing."

The exception to this is the period, which does not appear in the quoted portion within the larger sentence.

"Rex gave me that 'Oh, I'm so tired' look."

The same holds true if the quoted remark concludes the utterance:

Has Rex given you that look that says, "Oh, I'm so tired"?

The phrasal adjective in this sentence might also be rendered hyphenated and without quotation marks instead.

"Rex gave me that oh-I'm-so-tired look."

Quotation Marks Used for Emphasis

Quotation marks can be used to show that a word is being handled, as Argentine writer David Viñas once vividly put it, "with tweezers."

"When Billy promised me an 'elegant' dinner, I didn't know he meant fast food."

———

"Now she says 'Roland' as if it were a contagious disease."

Again, this can get a little tricky, as in the following example:

"What do you mean, 'inexcusable'?"

Here, *inexcusable* is a word lifted from a declaration ("His conduct was inexcusable"), so the single quotation marks are closed *before* the final mark of punctuation, which here governs the larger response, which is a question.

Some writers prefer to create this "tweezerliness" by using italics instead of single quotation marks.

"What do you mean, *inexcusable?*"

This is up to you. Just don't use both single quotation marks *and* italics.

Overuse of Quotation Marks for Emphasis

Perhaps influenced by critical or journalistic work that they have done, some apprentice writers feel obligated to place every colloquialism or technical term between quotation marks. This slows down the reader and draws unnecessary attention to the words themselves.

Bob felt like a total "dork." He hadn't really meant to "deep-six" the information when he "rebooted" the computer. Now, Mr. Lafferty would be "ticked off" at him, and he would probably never get to work "graveyard" again.

Enough already!

Quotations Within Quotations Within Quotations

Finally, for a doozy of a closer on this subject, when writing a quotation within a quotation within a quotation, alternate double and single quotation marks.

"As Robert put it, alluding to Poe, 'Quoth the Raven, "Nevermore." ' "

THOUGHTS

Recently, tremendous confusion has arisen about how to set **characters' thoughts**. (Writers sometimes seem to just make things difficult for themselves.) There are a number of tried-and-true ways to approach this issue.

Paraphrase

A character's thinking is often simply integrated into the narrative itself by means of **paraphrase**. In the following example, we don't actually hear the words that Tom is forming in his head; instead we get a paraphrase—a restatement—of them, as is obvious by the use of the third-person pronoun (*he, him*), rather than the first-person pronoun (*I, me*).

As Tom walked down the street, he thought about how silly the whole incident now seemed. What had possessed him to bring the subject up? And if he had, why did Muriel pursue it? Oh, well, that was water under the bridge now.

Arriving at the station, he bought his ticket and sighed. He had to wait forty-five minutes before his train arrived.

This traditional manner of transmitting a character's thoughts is clear, efficient, and familiar to readers. In many works, it is the only technique you need to use.

Quoted Thoughts

Some writers prefer, however, to actually **quote** Tom's thoughts, and this is where things can get complicated. If the publisher's house style permits it, it's acceptable, when employing the verb *thought*, to frame what your character is literally thinking with quotation marks.

As Tom walked down the street, he thought, "The whole incident seems silly now. What possessed me to bring the subject up? And why did Muriel pursue it? Oh, well, that's water under the bridge now."

Arriving at the station, he bought his ticket and sighed. He had to wait forty-five minutes before his train arrived.

You can argue that, in the foregoing, it's clear that what is between the quotation marks represents what is going through Tom's mind. Both the tense and the pronouns in those sentences are different than those in the surrounding narrative, and there's the overt presence of the verb *thought* as well. Are the quotation marks even necessary? Beyond this, a very strong case can be made that, in order to avoid confusion, quotation marks should be reserved solely for words that are actually uttered.

If you chose to eliminate the quotation marks, however, you probably want to replace the comma following the verb *thought* with a stronger mark of punctuation, either a dash or, even better, a colon.

As Tom walked down the street, he thought: The whole incident seems silly now. What possessed me to bring the subject up? And why did Muriel pursue it? Oh, well, that's water under the bridge now.

Arriving at the station, he bought his ticket and sighed. He had to wait forty-five minutes before his train arrived.

SINGLE AND DOUBLE QUOTATION MARKS

Some authors try to distinguish between quotations of speech and those of thoughts by employing double quotation marks for the former and single quotation marks for the latter.

"See you all later," Tom called as he closed the door.

As Tom walked down the street, he thought, 'The whole incident seems silly now. What possessed me to bring the subject up?'

This is not an attractive option. If thought and utterance are intermingled or fall hard upon one another, asking the reader to note the difference between double and single quotation marks is a bit much.

THOUGHTS IN ITALICS

Another commonly employed technique is **setting thoughts in italics** to emphasize that the reader is inside the character's head. This is especially useful when thought and narrative are interspersed with each other.

"See you all later," Tom called as he closed the door.

As Tom walked down the street, he could hardly make out the houses through the dark. *The whole incident seems silly now.* Once or twice, he stumbled on the uneven pavement. *What possessed me to bring the subject up? And why did Muriel pursue it?* He was not even sure he was headed in the right direction, but he pressed on anyway.

Arriving at the station, he bought his ticket and sighed. *Oh, well, that's water under the bridge now.* He had to wait forty-five minutes before his train arrived.

This variation in type style leaves little doubt as to what is narrative, what is dialogue, and what is thought. This method has become more and more standard over the last hundred years and is probably the preferable option.

ONE OTHER NOTE

As long as we're talking about thinking, remember that thought is a solitary activity conducted in silence. Hence, if somebody is thinking aloud, go ahead and say so.

Brendan began thinking out loud. "But what if we just pretended we never told her?"

However, it's simply redundant to write

Brendan thought to himself, "But what if we just pretended we never told her?"

Unless he's in some alternate universe, who else would Brendan be thinking to?

11

Other Issues of Usage

NUMBERS

For numbers, should writers use numerals or words or both? Generally, numbers should be spelled out as long as they are relatively simple. What's relatively simple? Opinions vary. In a scientific paper or a sociology article that contains tight columns of statistics, numerals are the rule. However, we're dealing here with creative texts, in which, presumably, the word enjoys a particularly privileged position.

Cardinal Numbers

Let's begin with **cardinal** numbers—the ones we use to count. Those up to one hundred and round numbers beyond one hundred are considered "simple" (e.g., "twelve," "fifty-four," "two hundred," "six billion," and so on). I'm inclined to follow the notion that numbers containing up to three elements should also be written out: "I've told you at least a hundred and forty-five times not to drop by!" You'll also note, in this example, the speaker says "a hundred," not "one hundred." That common practice is not apparent in the numeric 145.

Then again, I'm not most editors, some of whom endorse numerals for any number greater than ten. To strike a happy medium: For numbers that are round ("five thousand"), write the words; for those that are not round, use words for numbers less than one hundred ("seventy-one") and numerals for those more than one hundred ("293"). In the end, the publisher's house style prevails.

In two-digit numbers greater than twenty, up to and including ninety-nine, separate the two elements with a hyphen ("forty-four," "eighty-nine"). Should you choose to write out a number of three digits or more, hyphenate only the part that would take a hyphen anyway, as in "one hundred thirty-eight," and "one thousand one hundred thirty-eight."

More complicated numbers should be rendered in Arabic numerals. Otherwise, they become clumsy to both write and read.

> "If you weren't desperate to replicate the results you got the first time, Dr. Blanchard, why did you repeat the experiment on 1,468 separate occasions?"

This also applies to sums of money. If the amount is straightforward, use words; if not, use numerals.

> For Elaine, it was a bargain at four dollars.

> _____

> She had earned exactly $1,214.83 in the previous three months.

As in the preceding, if you use the word for the currency involved (*dollars*, *pounds*, and so on), express the quantity in words. If you employ the symbol of the currency ($, £), employ numerals.

Simple fractions ("one-quarter," "one-half") should be rendered with words; more complicated ones, with numerals.

> With two-thirds the effort, she proved 99/100 more efficient.

Ordinal Numbers

These same rules apply, more or less, to **ordinal** numbers (e.g., "first," "second," "third," and so on). "He was the third person to call" is correct over "He was the 3rd person to call", as is "I met her on the twenty-third of October" over " . . . on the 23rd of October." In cases like these, a writer would obviously opt for words rather than numerals. However, when the ordinal is complicated ("He was the two thousand one hundred and ninety-first person to call"), it makes more sense to employ numerals ("the 2,191st person"). Spelling the number out would never be incorrect, but it is awkward.

Streets and Addresses

"Forty-ninth Street," "Fifth Avenue," and "Seven Mile Road" can be rendered as "49th Street," "5th Avenue," and "7 Mile Road." Still, I'm inclined to use words rather than numerals for such street names.

Addresses on these streets, however, should always be rendered with numerals—"1 Fifth Avenue," "2926 Seven Mile Road"—simply because that's how we conventionally display an address. An exception to this might occur for a business that employs its address as its name, though only when the entity itself uses words rather than numerals.

> "We met at Eighty-One Fourteen Marsden, a very trendy club that had opened in September on the East Side."

Conventional Use of Numerals

The use of numerals is standard in instances in which we typically read or envision something in figures—telephone numbers, zip codes, Social Security numbers, interest rates, measurements, some e-mail addresses, page numbers, highways, trains known by their hour of departure, airline flights, track and gate numbers, aisles in a store, radio stations, television channels, and so on.

> "Call me at 555-2405."

> "My account was only paying 2.7%."

> Myrtle was assigned room 1104, the Royal Suite.

> His handle was ZipDrive501.

> "Mickey hadn't the vaguest notion what a 401(k) was."

> "Go up the 308 freeway and you'll see the station on your left. If you hurry, you'll have no problem meeting the 10:03."

> "There's a special on toilet paper over on aisle 14."

I was trying to listen to 104.3, but she insisted on turning on the Channel 8 news.

———

The Mark of the Beast is 666.

House styles differ here. Some publishers prefer, for example, "2.7 percent" as opposed to "2.7%," or "aisle fourteen" over "aisle 14." For your manuscript, a most important thing—as ever—is to be consistent (i.e., don't use "2.7 percent" on page twelve and "90%" on page eighteen).

Height, Weight, and Dimensions

Here, unsurprisingly, a degree of common sense goes a long way. A writer of creative prose is not a journalist, who is on a deadline and is concerned with the number of keystrokes involved in rendering numbers. A creative writer is not limited to a certain number of column inches, so the number of spaces a word takes as opposed to a numeral is not significant. What follows are some general suggestions for dealing with the presentation of height, weight, and dimensions.

When describing height that is simple or approximate, employ words.

Sally was around five feet tall.

If, however, you are going to give us Sally's exact height, use numerals, along with the standard symbolic abbreviations for feet and inches.

Sally was 5′ 1¾″ tall.

My preference for this is based on the rule put forth regarding currency: Words go with words, and symbols (which is what numerals are) go with symbols. Opinions differ on this. Some would find it entirely appropriate to write "5 feet, 1¾ inches," though nobody would endorse "five′ one and three-quarters″ " or, for that matter, "5 ft. 1¾ ins." It is also correct to employ the words alone: "five feet, one and three-quarters inches tall."

I've noted elsewhere that this kind of absolute accuracy is not especially useful in creative work. Our capacity to make an eyeball distinction between five feet and 5′ 1¾″ is virtually nil. Such exactitude is often a waste of time.

Where weight is concerned, follow the rule stated above. Spell out numbers less than and including one hundred, and spell out round numbers. With more complex quantities, use numerals.

> Mildred had shrunk to eighty-eight pounds.
>
> ----
>
> Bob had ballooned to 268 pounds.

Avoid the use of the abbreviations *lbs.* and *oz.* These simply don't save enough space to be worth the trouble.

With dimensions of an object, a room, a piece of property, and so on, follow these same standards.

> The old chest was two feet by three feet.
>
> ----
>
> The room measured 15′ 9″ by 11′ 7½″.

We visualize the expressions for certain things in terms of numerals. For these, use numerals on the page. For example:

> He constructed the fence entirely of 2 × 4s.

Remember, however, that these are ultimately questions of style, not strict rules. Writing 15′ 9″ × 11′ 7½″ or "two by fours" is not incorrect. What is significant is, once you have made a stylistic choice, that you stick with it.

Years and Dates

Years and **dates** including the year should be written as follows:

> "It was the worst storm since 1925."
>
> ----
>
> "I met her on October 23, 1987."

On the last example, it is left to the reader to add the ordinal suffix *-rd* when reading "October 23." That is, she will hear in her head "October twenty-third" rather than "October twenty-three," just as she hears "nineteen twenty-five," not "one thousand nine hundred twenty-five."

Time of Day

Time can be a problem, especially now that digital clocks give us very exact numbers. We used to commonly say it was "about half past five," whereas now we glance at our watches and say, "It's five thirty-two."

It is also acceptable to write "It's 5:32," though I would balk at "a quarter to 5:00" or even at "5:30" merely because, in creative work, words would do just as well for such simple expressions. Still, a lot of editors would accept "5:30" without a second thought.

It is incorrect to write "It's 5." If you insist on using numerals for time, then use the colon and indicate the minutes, even though they're "00," as in "It's 5:00."

The abbreviations for *ante meridiem* and *post meridiem* ("before midday" and "after midday") are usually written in lowercase with periods—a.m. and p.m. They can also be capitalized (A.M. and P.M.). Printers often render these abbreviations in "small caps" (A.M. and P.M.), which you may or may not be able to do on your computer.

Never Start a Sentence With Any Kind of Numeral

The following is unacceptable:

Sandy was very relieved. 145 people attended the show.

The second sentence should be

One hundred forty-five people attended the show.

If you have a complicated number—something not round but decidedly specific—at the beginning of a sentence, rework the sentence so the numerals do not fall at the outset. The following examples illustrate correct form:

Sam received 1,223,401 responses from Rotarians all over the world.

———

The year 1967 was a difficult one for Brad.

These versions should not be used.

1,223,401 Rotarians responded to Sam's international poll.

————

1967 was a difficult year for Brad.

Other Numerals

The only other numbers likely to appear in creative prose are **Roman numerals**: I = 1, V = 5, X = 10, L = 50, C = 100, and so on. These crop up as part of a person's name or title, where it would also be acceptable to spell out the word ("Louis XIV" or "Louis the Fourteenth" or, if you want to be really precise, "Louis Quatorze"). This applies, as well, to renderings of particular events ("World War I" or "World War One" or "the First World War").

ABBREVIATIONS

Unlike numerals, which are symbols, abbreviations are shortened versions of words. Abbreviations are usually made up of the initial letters of each word in a compound word or a few letters from a single word. These can signify an organization ("FBI" for "Federal Bureau of Investigation"), a common scholarly expression (often foreign in origin, such as "i.e." for *id est*, Latin for "that is"), a unit of measurement ("lbs." for "pounds," from the Latin *libra*), and so on. An abbreviation is not the same thing as a "clipped word," a contracted form of some longer word which is actually pronounced as a word in and of itself. *Memo* is a clipped word from *memorandum*; *pub* from *public house*. The clipped word *kilo* comes from *kilogram*, which is abbreviated "kg."

The use and form of abbreviations in your creative work are determined by the "speech test." If you read your sentence aloud, what do you actually *say*?

For example, your car has a speedometer that measures your speed in miles per hour (m.p.h.) and a tachometer that measures the rotation speed of the engine's crankshaft in revolutions per minute (r.p.m.). Let's say that when you were thirteen, your aunt Loretta decided to take Cousin Floyd's Corvette out for a spin.

Her foot felt like it was made of cement. She simply couldn't lift it from the accelerator. Glancing below the dashboard, she realized the car was moving at over 125 miles per hour, and the Good Lord knew what all those r.p.m.s meant!

If you were telling this story to someone, you would say "miles per hour," not "m.p.h." Likewise, what would come out of your mouth is "r.p.m.s," not "revolutions per minute." That is simply convention. The same reasoning is behind not using, for example, the abbreviation "lbs." in a story. We say "pounds," not "lubs" (or however you'd pronounce it) or "*libras.*"

You can simply intuit, in most instances, whether to employ an abbreviation or not, though there are glaring exceptions to the rule we just stated. When was the last time your wrote "Misses" for "Mrs." or "Doctor" for "Dr." when these were used as forms of address attached to a proper name—"Mrs. Randall, "Dr. Crane"? Coming upon "etc." in a sentence, we say "et cetera," the Latin for "and so on." Yet, we virtually never see it written out.

In that last case, you can avoid the "etc." problem. Perhaps it will appear in dialogue ("So she kept nagging me: Take out the trash, mow the lawn, weed the flowers, etc., etc., etc."), but, in narrative, the term looks vague and lazy. Besides, English has some pretty straightforward phrases that accomplish the same thing "etc." does—"and so on," "and the like," (ahem) etc.

PARAGRAPHING AND WHITE SPACE

In fiction, use **indentation** to indicate a new paragraph. Do not use block paragraphing—skipping a space between paragraphs and keeping the first line flush left—which is employed in business correspondence, flyers, and the like.

Dear Sirs:
I am writing to complain about the service I received at Marco's Italian Kitchen on 26 August.

On arriving at the restaurant, my party was subjected to inexcusable delays in both seating and service.

You avoid this because "white space" (when you double-space the type, this is three line spaces instead of one) is often used to cue the reader that some kind of change is occurring in your story. Editors call this a topic break. When you encounter a white space while reading, you know that something is going to be different when you start the next paragraph—the location has shifted, time has passed, the narrator (or narrative center) of the upcoming action is different than it has been up to this point. The following illustrates a shift in time (from night to the following morning), place (from Rhonda's bedroom to Andrew's car), and point of view (from Rhonda to Andrew).

Rhonda snuggled deeper under the covers, and, with hardly another thought of Andrew, was soon fast asleep.

On his drive to work at seven-fifteen sharp, Andrew felt his regrets about the previous night pounding in his head.

Were this passage to fall at the same point as a page break, just to be certain that the reader realized there was a white space here (which may not be obvious), you would insert three, centered "wingdings" or "dingbats" (usually asterisks) either at the bottom of one page or the top of the other, like this:

Rhonda snuggled deeper under the covers, and, with hardly another thought of Andrew, was soon fast asleep.

* * *

On his drive to work at seven-fifteen sharp, Andrew felt his regrets about the previous night pounding in his head.

ITALICS (AND OTHER ODD TYPE STYLES)

Keep the use of varying type styles to a minimum in your manuscript. It's not incorrect to employ them, but they can become a crutch and often are merely unnecessary. If a sentence is written effectively, the kind of emphasis that *italics* or **boldface** is supposed to supply is simply inherent—that is, the stress the odd typeface signals is already there.

"What kind of person do you think I *am*!"

Why italicize that last word when we would normally stress it in this sentence? To emphasize a word the reader wouldn't stress, italicize it.

"What kind of person *do* you think I am!"

However, it may be possible to imply in the context and sentence construction where this unusual emphasis falls.

"I didn't think you were that kind of person."
"Well, just what kind of person do you think I am!"

I think you'll agree that the syntax and word choice in this exchange naturally throw the stress in the second sentence onto "do" and thus eliminate the need for italics.

Words and Conversations in Foreign Languages

You sometimes can employ italics without fretting. You should italicize foreign words or phrases: *che será, será*; *zeitgeist*; *amigo mío*; *mon frère*. You should not, however, italicize certain common expressions that have, practically speaking, become English words: "per diem," "hubris," "pathos," "objet d'art," and so on. Also, proper names, place names, businesses, and so on, are *not* italicized: "Charlemagne," "Mao Tse-Tung," "Nuevo Laredo," "Via Veneto," "La Alhambra," "Frankfurter-Platz," "Le Cirque."

In your writing, you may employ sentences or even conversations uttered in a foreign language. Thomas Mann has an entire chapter in *The Magic Mountain* (written in German) in which the dialogue is in French. This shows the level of erudition he anticipated in his audience, but that seems a bit much for us in the contemporary world!

In such instances, employ quotation marks and italics with the words in the foreign language that characters utter, and then either translate them into English in your narrative, or, even better, append a narrative detail that will illuminate for the reader the significance of the foreign phrase.

Maryanne handed a cupcake to Madame Harange. *"Pour vous."* For you.
Tentatively, the old woman took a bite. *"Quelle fantastiqué!"* she exclaimed and then rapidly devoured the entire pastry.

Titles of Works

Italics are also always called for when referring to long (book-length) works of fiction, nonfiction, poetry, and drama (*Absalom, Absalom*; *The Fire Next*

Time; *Paradise Lost*; *An Enemy of the People*); magazines and newspapers (*Newsweek*, *The New York Times*); films and television series (*All About Eve*, *Nightline*); album-length recordings (*The Immaculate Collection*); ballets, operas, and titled instrumental compositions (*Romeo and Juliet*, *Norma*, *Rhapsody in Blue*, but *not* Schubert's Symphony in C Major); paintings and sculptures (*The Raft of the Medusa*, Michelangelo's *David*); and, finally, ships, aircraft, and named trains (RMS *Titanic*, the *Spirit of St. Louis*, the *Twentieth Century Limited*).

Oddly enough, the Bible and its books (Genesis, I Corinthians) are simply capitalized. This is true of all other sacred writings (the Quran, the Torah, the Upanishads, and so on).

If you are still using a typewriter rather than a computer, indicate italics by underlining, as in <u>An Enemy of the People</u> and <u>Newsweek</u>. Do *not*, however, employ both, as in <u>*The Fire Next Time*</u>, the <u>*Twentieth Century Limited*</u>. This is incorrect.

SHORTER WORKS

Titles of shorter works (chapters, short stories, short poems, one-act plays, individual essays, articles and editorials, episodes, songs—virtually anything that would normally appear as a **part** or **section** of a larger work) are flanked by quotation marks, as in "We Are Introduced . . . ," "My Old Man," "Kublai Khan," "The Zoo Story," "Bush's Dilemma," "Captain Kirk Strikes Out," "Material Girl."

Other Literary Uses of Italics

As noted in chapter ten, italics are often employed to indicate thoughts or to differentiate a particular passage in the text from other parts of the text. Remember?

> As Tom walked down the street, he could hardly make out the houses through the dark. *The whole incident seems silly now.* Once or twice, he stumbled on the uneven pavement. *What possessed me to bring the subject up? And why did Muriel pursue it?* He was not even sure he was headed in the right direction, but pressed on anyway.
>
> How could he ever forget those words: *"Get out! And don't ever darken my doorstep again!"*

Sometimes, onomatopoeic words are italicized.

> She strained her ears. Was she really hearing anything? *Tap. Tap. Tap.* There it was! She listened even harder. *Tap. Tap. Tap.* There was no question now.

Don't become too fond of variant type faces. We can do to a manuscript all kinds of funny things that were once virtually impossible. Beyond italics, you should avoid using any of those snazzy effects your computer can generate. **Boldface**, o̶u̶t̶l̶i̶n̶e̶, SMALL CAPS, and so on are simply affectations in narrative and are more appropriate to flyers and brochures than to stories. In the end, it is your words that are significant. Your emphases and nuances and ironies should be apparent in and of themselves, not because you futzed around in the "format" function of your computer.

REGARDING YOUR COMPUTER

All magic comes at a price.

Home computers and word processors make possible all kinds of things that, even in the eighties, once required long hours to accomplish or were impossible to accomplish at all. Many present-day writers have never really typed a final draft; taking a manuscript replete with editing marks and retyping the whole thing from scratch. Yet, that is precisely what writers of all kinds used to do every day.

This is, frankly, a good idea, in that it allows for a kind of "touch edit" of your work. Your fingers may note a word repeated in two successive sentences when your eye may miss it. Honestly, I suggest that you completely retype your final draft, though I suspect the chances of this advice being taken is almost nil. (I can almost hear the "yeah, right!")

A Quick Note on Margins

Most editors still prefer a **right margin** that's "ragged," *not* "justified." Justification may make a piece of work look pretty, but it can complicate the jobs of editors and typesetters, who generally can look at a page of typed text and mentally determine how it will appear on the printed page. That appearance can vary wildly depending on the font that is used, page dimensions, and so on.

This preference of the ragged right style may change as more and more publications ask that writers provide work not only in hard copy, but also on disk. Nonetheless, at present, the way text looks on a typed or printed manuscript and the way it gets set in a particular publication (where it probably *will* have a justified right margin) differ, and it is not up to the writer to do the typesetting.

Printing Drafts

In any case, with computer-generated text, print at least one rough draft and edit it by hand. As the years go by and people learn from the first grade to compose text on-screen, the following may not be true, but, presently, you simply see things more clearly on the page than you can on your monitor. After this edit, make the corrections and emendations on the computer file.

Check Grammar and Spelling

Do not rely on your computer's grammar and spelling checkers. You may write an apparently grammatical sentence that makes no sense in the context of the paragraph. Likewise, your program may constantly tell you that your sentences are too long or too short. This may be, but, because of the story you're telling or the style you've adopted, long sentences or choppiness may be exactly what you want. Imagine what a computerized grammar check would do with a novel by Alain Robbe-Grillet or E.L. Doctorow! It's certainly okay to employ this function to detect egregious errors, but don't depend entirely on it.

With the spelling checker, remember that the machine can catch only misspellings resulting in words that don't exist ("blok" for "block," for example). It will not catch all typos (e.g., "you" where you meant to write "your") or misused homonyms ("There" swing is on "they're" porch over "their"). Further, many words in English are anagrams of other words. You may want to say, "John won the game." However, you could mistype "won" as "now," "own," "wont," "wan," "want," "went, "town" "win" and so on. All of these are proper English words, and your spelling checker will read past them without the slightest pause.

Despite these advisories, both of these functions on the computer can be quite useful. Your spelling checker will catch errors in orthography (e.g., "mispell") and some of the typos we all are prone to (ever typed "hte" as an article?). Likewise, the grammar checker will alert you to instances that trip up all of us now and then—repeated sentence structures, sentence fragments, run-on sentences, and the like. Think of these checkers as a fourth grade teacher from 1958—somebody who really, truly knows the rules but may not be highly attuned to the nuances of style and voice.

Take It Slow!

Whatever you do, do not rush when employing these tools your machine provides. A couple of years back, I read a story involving a highly complicated affair between a young woman and a man who turned out to be a priest. The plot had multiple twists and turns, and the heroine, Addie, was in a state of almost constant romantic angst before the changing attitudes of her mysterious suitor. The writer obviously worked on the piece right up to the last minute, and, though apparently satisfied with the first half, she had some reservations about the second. It seems she ran her spelling checker without really keeping track of what it was correcting. How could I tell? Along about page 7, the name Addie was suddenly (perhaps appropriately, but rather confusingly for the reader), transformed into Addled, and it remained so throughout the rest of the text.

Even if you don't have a workshop due date for a story, you can lose patience with what you are working on and birth it before it is due. Cut yourself some slack. Rome was not built in a day, nor was Dante's *La Commedia* written in a month. It's true Georg Freidrich Handel wrote his *Messiah* in a couple of weeks, but if you listen to his earlier work, you can hear how he'd been tweedling with a lot of those themes for a long, long time—the ones that turned up as "Every Valley . . . " and "The Trumpet Shall Sound," and the "Hallelujah!" chorus.

Be kind to yourself. You don't have to be *The Night of the Iguana*'s poor rector, who spends his entire life trying to write a perfect sonnet and then expires as soon as he finally accomplishes the task. But, allow for the fact that, if you wait a day or a week or a month, you can recognize virtues and flaws in your text that, on an immediate rereading, might be impossible to identify.

One downside of the new technologies is that we expect them to make our narratives as perfect in content as we can make the form on the printed page. This notion is an illusion. In the end, your story—real or fictional—can only be as worked and elegant and moving as you make it.

Some Final Thoughts

Before the advent of personal computers in the early eighties, a great deal more sheer labor was involved in writing anything. These machines we all use have revolutionized the way we produce texts, the way we edit them, the way we receive them. It is plausible that the impact of the computer on humankind in our age will prove, historically, to be equivalent to that of Gutenberg's printing press in the Fifteenth Century.

Practically, however, the computer bears with it certain problems. So far as your machine is concerned, your beautifully composed and orchestrated text is nothing but a series of 0s and 1s. Your capacity to instantly delete a passage you decide you don't like means—at least for those who are not versed in the various ways of information retrieval—that it is gone forever. Beyond this, there are those dreaded power surges, power failures, viruses, and so on, that can obliterate hours' or weeks' or months' worth of work in the flickering of an eye. I still remember encountering, a couple of years back, a very reserved, though always cheerful Korean graduate student who had tears welling in his eyes. Half of his dissertation had, in an instant, simply vanished one evening. A computer crash, in this electronic age, can be as devastating to your work as a house fire.

Set your machine to automatically "save" material, and "back up" your work frequently. That way, should the worst occur—a lightning strike fifteen miles away turns your latest magnum opus into the cyberspace equivalent of ash—you will at least have a record of some of the text that has been fried. This grim possibility is yet another reason to print, from time to time, a hard copy of your work. This can be the difference between simply reconstructing the skeleton of that story or novel or essay that is destined to make you a star and starting all over again.

In addition, writers sometimes simply repent their overenthusiastic editing. A word or phrase or an entire paragraph may seem, at three in the morning, extraneous, but the next day or a week later, you may realize it was essential, lending a certain nuance to a passage that you had missed entirely in your predawn bleariness. Zapped by the "delete" key, it's gone forever.

An old rule among writers says you should never throw any writing away. Admittedly, this means a writer has paper up the wazoo. It can reach the point where, even if you seem to recall a brilliant piece of description you cut from a work three years ago, you won't for the life of you be able to remember where you put it. Nonetheless, be cautious. Your computer doesn't refer to that place on your desktop screen as "trash" or the "recycle bin" for nothing. Tossing a passage or page in there means that, as sure as if you hustled the garbage down to corner just as the sanitation truck was making its rounds, it's lost when you command the machine to "empty" the trash.

Beyond this, think of the future. When writers had to laboriously recopy their texts by hand or, later on, run them one more time through the type-writer, they left a record of how works evolved. We can see how Henry James shaped and honed *The Princess Casamassima* or how T.S. Eliot revised *The Wasteland* thanks to those rough drafts in longhand or typed on foolscap that are still extant in libraries throughout the world. If nothing else, these primitive versions of great works have provided scholars a means of seeing how genius functions, how tinkering with a word here and a phrase there transformed something that was merely good into an immortal gem.

Do those poor graduate students of the future a favor!

Ten Issues of Language and Style

Introduction to Language and Style

Part I dealt with issues of grammar and mechanics. Part II focuses on some larger questions of language and style. Its ten short chapters address topics ranging from the use of jargon to the sources of metaphor. Some of these matters, such as offensive language, are fraught with controversy; others demand that we get somewhat technical, as is the case in the discussion of dialect in your prose.

While what follows is far from an exhaustive exploration of language and style, in my experience, these are the topics that most frequently arise in workshops. From each of the chapters, you should be able to garner enough advice to make informed decisions on these particular issues. For creative prose to work, it has to go beyond mere mechanical correctness. You describe settings, you choose images, you name your characters, you employ allusions: How you do all these profoundly affects how your story is received. An inappropriate metaphor or a slip in historical accuracy can ruin a piece in that it breaks the contract between writer and reader. If your reader stumbles because, for example, you've included a cell phone in a story set in 1980, then you've probably lost her for good. If she can't trust your knowledge of the era you write about, why should she trust you to accurately portray the emotions of the characters you've created?

As you'd probably expect, there are few hard-and-fast rules regarding any of these topics. Clichés, for example, which you might think should always be eschewed, may be exactly what you want in your text. Furthermore, though a reader wouldn't anticipate an Italian-American character named Alister, it's entirely legitimate to create one as long as you offer some explanation as to why he is Alister rather than Angelo. Indeed, this apparent anomaly might add complexity and nuance to his character and circumstances.

Enjoy what follows. Certainly, these are issues that writers constantly discuss and disagree over. After you've finished this section, you should be more than ready to enter into the fray.

12

Titles and Names

TITLES

Issues that frequently arise in workshops are those of titling stories and naming characters. Interestingly enough, writers tend to fret more about the former than the latter, though I would argue—generally at least—that they have their priorities reversed. No one can deny that a work's title is tremendously important. Can you imagine admiring *Trimalchio* as the quintessential portrait of the Jazz Age with quite the same intensity as we admire *The Great Gatsby*? Yet, the former was F. Scott Fitzgerald's working title, and it was not entirely inappropriate, alluding as it does to the party animal created by the Roman writer Petronius Arbiter in his racy romance of the First Century, *The Satyricon*. Thomas Wolfe's *Look Homeward, Angel*—titled from a quotation from John Milton's great poem of mourning, "Lycidas"—began life with the rather generic and melodramatic title *O Lost*.

The fact is that a writer often won't know precisely what to call a piece until he's done with it and has had the chance to see where it ended up, which may well be a different place than the writer had imagined originally. I wrote a book that I originally called *Memory Tapes*. When the first draft was done, my agent pointed out that she found the title misleading because it implied that the tone of the book would be much more conversational than it was. She anticipated swatches in which the central characters would speak as if into a tape recorder, as if keeping some kind of oral diary.

Casting around for something different, I settled on *American Century*. Henry Luce, the publisher of *Time* magazine, had used this term in 1946 to describe the Twentieth Century, and, given that the action of the book traversed the years from World War II to the mid nineties, it seemed an appropriate choice for my novel.

Other people disagreed, finding it clunky and pretentious. The book was literally on its way to the printer before my editor and I agreed on a title, one that made absolute sense. In the novel, there is a dress shop, "Letting Loose," that carries somewhat outrageous fashions. Initially, that mundane provenance—the name of a store—hardly seemed appropriate for my attempt at the Great American Novel. The more my editor explained his idea, however, and the more I thought about, it was simply right. The story is one about people moving into middle age; making peace with the ways their lives have gone; "letting loose" of a whole set of notions and beliefs and griefs and enmities that appeared central to their very identities when they were younger, just as, in those earlier years, they had once "let loose" of their conventional moorings.

Circumstances vary. Sometimes, a writer knows precisely what the title is before ever committing a single word to paper. Other times, the writer ends up just as frantic as I was. The lesson to be learned from my experience (and those of Wolfe and Fitzgerald, for that matter) is that often an outsider can see beyond alternatives you have been juggling and find the right name for a text, one that never occurred to the author. Your agent, your editor, and writers in your workshop or writing group are good people to turn to, even if you think you have the title you want.

Allow yourself to use a "working title"—a name you don't feel entirely satisfied with that, nonetheless, gives your piece a tentative identity. Over time, it may grow on you, or you may come up with something more fitting. Argentine writer Roberto Mariani, as he wrote his stories, had different ideas of what his text should be called as it developed. He jotted each down on a scrap of paper and tossed these in his desk drawer. When he finished a story, he noted which of the these titles he remembered first. That one became the story's title.

A stray piece of interesting information is that, though texts can be copyrighted, titles cannot. If you want to call your book *Hamlet* or *Moby Dick* or *The Shining* or *The Voyage of the Narwhal,* legally, no one can stop you. Of course, this may not be the greatest idea, and an editor is likely to do her best to dissuade you. Note, though, that Miguel de Cervantes and Kathy Acker each published a novel called *Don Quixote.* Also in Acker's body of work is a book entitled *Great Expectations.*

CHARACTER NAMES

While writers obsess rather too much about titles, they sometimes don't obsess enough about the names of their characters. As I never tire of repeating, few stories work well when characters are *not* named. Calling your protagonists "he" and "she" merely makes them seem generic rather than universal. There are exceptions to this, but the plain truth is that the very first thing we do when we meet someone is exchange names. Your name provides you an identity, and this is no less true of imagined people than it is of real ones.

The happy truth is that, nine times out of ten, characters already know what their names are when they first pop into our imaginations. The best-known illustration of this tenth time is the fiery Scarlett O'Hara, who, in the first draft of *Gone With the Wind*, had what now seems the absurdly incongruous moniker of "Pansy" O'Hara.

In the larger context of your story, names can be problematic. Be cautious, in general, of using names that have a similar sound. I read an apprentice story in which the major secondary characters were Ken and Kevin, which made it difficult for the reader to keep straight precisely who was who, especially in that the latter was sometimes addressed as "Kev." The protagonist's two friends simply bled into each other. You could argue that, with strong enough characterizations, this would not have been a problem. This implies, however, that the author would have had to spend time and space early on in his tale making the distinction between the pair obvious—this time and space are better spent on other matters. In sum, simply turning Ken into Tom cuts the Gordian knot and allows the writer to concentrate on what is truly significant in his story.

After the first couple drafts of the aforementioned *Letting Loose*, Basil, an expatriate Englishman teaching at the local community college, became Malcolm. For some reason, I have a weakness for names that begin with *B*. Already in the novel, I had major characters named Belva, Barry, Bobbo, and Bowan, along with two others whose last names were Bowdin and Bower. Frankly, I maybe ought to have thought about changing a couple of other names as well!

Still, that's often hard to do with a fictional person, because you think of that character with the name she first appeared within your imagination. Like anybody else, characters hold on with remarkable ferocity to what they are christened with. Indeed, both my editor and I were so accustomed to "Basil" that the printed text includes a "ghost," one moment when we both slipped up and Malcolm was suddenly back to his birth name.

On the other hand, there may be a legitimate reason for characters to have similar or even identical names. I feature in a couple of my novels a pair of twins whose names are Belva and Melva. Gabriel García Márquez's *One Hundred Years of Solitude* includes what seems like innumerable Aurelianos and José Arcadios, precisely because this serves a larger thematic purpose: Despite the passage of time, residents of the village of Macondo continue to repeat the errors of their progenitors, just as, over and over, generations of them bear the same names. Keep in mind, however, that García Márquez's book comes complete with a genealogy to help readers keep everybody straight.

A common problem with stories set in the past is characters whose names seem odd in that era. Names, like everything else, go in and out of fashion. In the last couple of decades, "Tiffany" has become relatively common for girls. It comes from Louis Tiffany, the American designer and jeweler who gave us, at the turn of the Twentieth Century, the Tiffany lamp and the famous store on Fifth Avenue. It would be quite unusual, however, to have a pigtailed tot, Tiffany, in a story set in 1932, much less in 1790. "Jared" and "Ian," or even "Sam" are relatively rare names among Americans born fifty years ago, though they are quite frequently shared among those born twenty years ago. Forty years back, "Zachary" would have been common only in the South or perhaps in New England, where boys were often given names that had been in the family for generations. Old Testament names—which, from the Sixteenth through the Nineteenth Centuries, were quite popular—such as "Eli," "Nathan," "Jacob," and "Jonah" fell almost entirely out of favor until the 1980s.

Names are often associated not only with particular moments in time but with regions, specific ethnic or religious groups, or even certain occupations or social classes. "Wesley," for example, appears in the South, particularly among Methodists, a Protestant denomination founded by John Wesley. Unsurprisingly, those names of prophets and Hebrew heroes mentioned in the previous paragraph never disappeared entirely from the Jewish community, while "Jesus," a very unusual name in English, is common (as "Jesús") in Spanish, as is "María" as part of a man's name (e.g., "José María," which translates to "Joseph Mary"). Readers would probably not be surprised that a truck driver's name is "Buck" or "Mel," but it might strike them as odd if he were the president of a Fortune 500 company or a career diplomat. This represents, of course, nothing but prejudices, in that there are probably truck drivers named Sebastian and CEOs named Gomer. You as a writer have to work around your audience's expectations—unfair though these may be. As a consequence, if a character's name doesn't jibe with these expectations, then you need to provide, even briefly, an explanation for why this character is so named.

Recently, African Americans have christened their children with historically African names ("Simba," "Ashanti") or newly coined ones ("Sherwonna," "DeShane"), but seventy-five years ago, this would have been rare. If they didn't choose conventional, largely English names ("Martin," "Ralph," "James," "Phillip"), African Americans favored Biblical ones ("Jesse," "Hosea," "Issac"). "Patrick" and "Michael" we associate with the Irish; "Carl" or "Gretchen," with Germans; "Sophia" and "Nicolas," with Greeks; "Ali" or "Hassan," with Arabs. "Nigel" strikes us as quintessentially British. Remember that many names are simply foreign variants of English ones. "Jan," "János," "João," "Jean," "Johann," "Juan," "Ian," "Ivan," and "Sean" are, respectively, the Polish, Hungarian, Portuguese, French, German, Spanish, Scottish, Russian, and Irish forms of "John." The names of opera composer Giuseppe Verdi—so ringingly Italian!—in his native land means "Joe Green."

This does not mean you can't have a New Mexican cowboy whose name is Hans or a Bulgarian washerwoman whose name is Molly. As we just noted, however, you will need to somehow justify this apparent anomaly: "Hans, great-grandson of a portly burgher in Dusseldorf . . . " or "The great love of Molly's father's life, he would insist when he was drunk, was a redheaded barmaid he had known when his ship docked in Dublin." Buck Siderski can be the president of International Mallet and Wicket or the American counsel in Bangkok if, somewhere along the line, the reader is informed of how this apparently peculiar circumstance came to pass.

Names tell us a great deal about who the characters are or what specific relationships are in a story. When we read "Yves came through the door," our immediate presumption is that he is French, just as, whether fairly or not, we assume until it is proven otherwise that a little girl named Jane is, well, plain. We make certain judgments about a character who insists that others address him as "Christopher" rather than "Chris." If characters in a novel call someone "Paul" but Mrs. Berkhardt calls him "Paulie," readers will assume she must have some particularly intimate relationship with him, whether somehow romantic or matronly. Characters relate differently among themselves just like real people do—formally or informally, as co-workers, as friends, as lovers. Kathryne Kerner may be "Ms. Kerner" at the office; "Miss Kerner" to the old German lady who runs the bakery; "Kathryne" to her father; "Katie" to her mother; "Kate" to her brother; "Kat" to her friends; and "Love Muffin" to her boyfriend, Norman.

What form a name takes can also indicate particular circumstances. If Norman suddenly addresses his love muffin as "Kathryne," there's probably something wrong. When a co-worker, let's say one who has recently gotten married, turns to her and pointedly says, "Well, Miss Kerner," we read this as catty. And if her mother says, "Kathryne Margaret Kerner!"—well, almost everyone I know recalls those moments when a parent called him not by his first name, but his full name. This meant one thing: big trouble!

Bear in mind that names have both a literal meaning and a historical and literary heritage. "Derek" is a Dutch diminutive of the orginally Greek "Theodore," "gift of God." "Kenneth" is "handsome" in Celtic, while "Oswald" is "divine power" in Old English. "Victor" is, well, "victor" in Latin, and "Cadwalader" (a new one for me) is "battle arranger" in Welsh. Women's names are no less diverse in their literal significance. "Audrey" comes to us from Germanic roots via Old French and means "noble might." "Enid" is Celtic for "purity." "Muriel" is "myrrh" in Greek. "Priscilla" means "ancient" in Latin; "Tabitha," "gazelle" in Aramaic.

Many people are probably ignorant of the original significance of most names, so baptizing your young genius of a hero "Cuthbert" ("notably brilliant" in Old English) is probably not going to tip off your reader from the get-go to the hero's intelligence. Further, even with names such as "Lily" or "Duke" we don't necessarily connect an individual with a flower or the ruler of a duchy. We are likely, however, to be conscious of a name's antecedents— at least some of them—whether in fact or fiction. "Adolf" rather lost its allure in the second half of the previous century, at least in those countries that were belligerents in World War II. Because of Benedict Arnold, the given name "Benedict" has never been especially popular in the United States, though the surname has not suffered the same fate. Melville's audience knew what he was about when in *Moby Dick* he chose to christen his main characters on the *Pequod* with the Biblical "Ishmael" ("the wanderer") and "Ahab" (the wicked

Israeli monarch in the Book of Kings). That may not have been the case, however, with the audience of Hemingway's *In Our Time*, in which the author's persona, Nick Adams, moves from innocence to experience with a name that combines that of the first man in the Garden of Eden with a slang term—as in "Old Nick"—for the devil.

Some names are so common and have so many associations that they cancel each other out. "Mary" is linked to both Christianity's virgin mother and, popularly if not scripturally, the Western World's most famous whore, Mary Magdalen. Still, if you baptize a character "Cassandra" or "Electra" or "Iago," you have to accept the fact that, at least for part of your audience, these folks are going to tote with them quite a load of baggage. That doesn't mean Cassie has to be one very frustrated clairvoyant or that Electra can't love her mom to death or that Iago isn't a hell of a guy. However, because of Homer and Aeschylus and Shakespeare, those names raise certain expectations that must be addressed, however subtly. Indeed, you can play with this sort of thing: Short-tempered and sharp-tongued Griselda can have absolutely nothing patient about her, while Byron can be thoroughly saintly and retiring. You can make a Marlowe who—unlike the Renaissance playwright Christopher or Raymond Chandler's Philip or Joseph Conrad's dispassionate narrator (with no first name and no *e* on the end of his last) in *Heart of Darkness*—is the very portrait of discretion, cheeriness, and optimism regarding all humankind.

We have talked thus far almost entirely about given names, but remember that surnames have meanings, ethnicities, histories, and literary antecedents as well. "Miller," like "Cooper" or "Smith," comes originally from a man's occupation—the one who ran the mill as opposed to the one who made barrels or the guy with the forge and anvil. If you set a story in a small French village, you have to explain why your protagonist is Mrs. Athanasiadas-Novas. Again, it isn't impossible for some Greek to have ended up by the Ardennes Forest, but you need to cue your audience as to why this is so.

In some ways, American writers and American settings are less bound by this sort of thing. The aforesaid "Miller," so very English, is, in fact, not an uncommon Jewish name, in that many immigrants had "native" surnames thrust upon them or they adopted the names on their own. "Fitzsimmons" became "Simmons," "Miklauski" became "Micklaus," "Andriotti" became "Andrews." Many contemporary Americans are such mongrels—a combination of so many different nationalities and races—that readers can accept a petite, green-eyed redhead as being Consuela Kuric without too much thought, however much that may violate preconceptions of what someone with a Spanish given name and Bosnian surname should look like.

Names can be tricky, but don't get yourself in a stew about them. Indeed, you can have a great deal of fun with names—the grim spinster who is Yvette or Chi-Chi; the three-hundred-pound, six foot-eight former fullback who goes by "Tiny" or "Scooter." Even as sacred a literary figure as William Faulkner must have had his giggles as he christened the wily and, on the whole, rapacious Snopeses—the tribe who displaces the *ancien régime* of Yoknapatawpha County—with names such as "Ab" (as in "Abbadon," the angel of the bottomless pit in Hell), "Flem" (as in phlegm?), "I.O." ("I owe") or the pornographer Montgomery Ward and his virtuous sibling, Wallstreet Panic Snopes.

13

Images

Ohe of the most personal and distinctive elements in your writing is the images you create. Despite this, we often don't think too much about them, paying too little attention to our figures of speech and their origins. The analogies we make between one thing and another are heavily determined by who we are and where we live and what our circumstances are. This is true of all aspects of our writing, but we often consider these issues more heavily when formulating our plots or characters than we do our imagery. Still, it is quite apparent that for readers "It was red as persimmons," "It was red as a hot Chevy roadster," and "It was red as a persimmon Chevy roadster" each evokes not only a different image but a different voice.

With that in mind, the first point to be made is that writers sometimes trip in their work by invoking an image that is out of sync with the story. We do not always narrate our own personal tales or set them in the reality that we exist in. If a protagonist lives in Hell's Kitchen in Manhattan, it makes perfect sense that his "heart soared as high and bright as the Chrysler Building." However, if he lives in rural Arizona, such a simile strikes a reader as odd. Our Westerner's heart would more likely "soar like a golden eagle in the summer sky."

This tripping is not as rare as it may sound. I've read numerous apprentice stories by suburbanites writing about the inner city, by inner-city people writing about the country, and by rural folks writing about both in which, throughout, something is "off." What makes it off is a lack of metaphor or a use of metaphors that don't fit with the place being evoked or the use of images that are canned—no more than precisely what we would expect. Readers don't anticipate that somebody in the city will smell "like a wet sheep," nor would they anticipate that someone's country house would have "all the charm of a fern bar." As always, especially in the Twenty-first Century, either of these might be entirely reasonable in a piece, but the author has to somehow prepare the audience for these unexpected intrusions of one world into another.

Writers also run the risk of erring in the opposite direction. They can draw in so many hard-boiled images when writing about the naked city or so many bucolic ones when writing about the great outdoors that readers get the sense that all the characters do is wander around noticing things around them in order to evoke them in connection with something else. In any use of image, find the means to seamlessly integrate your metaphors into your text so that their very presence will contribute power and texture.

TYPES OF FIGURATIVE LANGUAGE

When we talk about images, we often think narrowly, tending to limit our consideration to "metaphor" in its strictist sense and to "simile." These are the real workhorses of figurative speech, and both imply comparison. In **simile**, the comparison is overt. Readers see that two different things, though not identical, are put forth as similar, literally "as" or "like" one another. These examples are similes.

"My love is like a red, red rose. . . . "
_____

"Brutus had a mouth like a shark's. . . . "
_____

"The smell was like a slaughterhouse's, but worse."

In **metaphor**, that difference vanishes. One element is simply equated with the other. Compare these metaphors to the similes.

"My love is a red, red rose. . . . "
_____

"He had a shark's mouth. . . . "
_____

"The smell was a slaughterhouse's."

Readers know—or should know—that the parallel established is, of course, not literally true. However, they realize that, figuratively, love is as soft and beautiful as that rose and that Brutus is probably not the nicest guy in the world.

Metaphor in its broader sense, however, lets us talk about figurative language more generally as well. Rhetoricians can go on endlessly about how we use words in ways that, though they allow a reader to comprehend what we intend, simultaneously escape the limits of mere observation or assertion. They convey things that are not, strictly speaking, what those words literally mean. Like simile and metaphor, some other types of figurative language are quite specific in their definitions, while still others are broader and have a variety of forms.

To expand on this, let's turn to **synecdoche** and **metonymy**. The former identifies instances in which a part of a larger whole stands stead for that whole itself, or, much less frequently, when an entirety stands stead for a part of itself. For example:

> There on the phone to Berlin, the Colonel suddenly went white. Still,
> he gave the order, and the dark helmets marched from house to house,
> plucking from each one family member—man or woman, boy or girl—
> for sacrifice to the outraged Goebbels.

Helmets, we know, are notoriously inept at getting around on their own. They really need to be sitting on somebody's noggin to get anyplace. Nonetheless, we understand that *helmets* here is standing stead for *Wehrmacht* or "troops" or "Nazis." A part of the uniform—in this instance, perhaps its most sinister and distinctive part—represents not only the uniform, but the soldier who wears it.

Now, let's take a stab at the opposite.

> The rooms of Lester's dormmates swung shut, one after another, as
> he slipped deeper and deeper into self-pity.

Here, it's apparent that we have to be referring to doors. You can see the power of the syndecdoche—not just the entrances but the spaces beyond them are being closed to Lester, and those spaces are inhabited by those he has been counting on to keep him emotionally afloat.

The same sort of thing happens with metonymy, however, the name of one thing is replaced not by a part of it but by something else closely associated with it. Readers see this quite commonly—just check the sports pages in the newspaper. Journalists speak of the rules of specific games—say, hockey or football—as those "of the rink" or "of the gridiron." In the editorial section, we hear about "dissident Capitol Hill" or "word from the White House." The hill can't dissent; the house can't speak. Still, readers understand that these are used in place of "dissident members of the House and Senate" or "what the president's spokesman says."

These kinds of metaphors allow writers to avoid repetition and to also draw attention to the specifics of virtually anything. Metaphor is about focus. It is about a certain, maybe terrifying, absoluteness. It allows you to go beyond the real and draw in those things that are thousands of years old or as present as anthrax in your mailbox. By its very comparison, the metaphor allows you to be intensely connected with both the elements that make it up.

There are other kinds of figurative language that, many times, writers don't even quite realize they are using. **Personification**, for example, attributes human characteristics to things animal, vegetable, or mineral, or about anything else.

> Pamela was so busy that she hardly noticed the Duluth spring making
> its usual stumbling, shambling entrance.

A season of the year cannot literally walk, talk, or crawl on its belly like a reptile. However, metaphorically, a lot of Minnesotans would surely agree that, in the far north of the Midwest, spring can make a number of false starts before it really gets the hang of things and strides forth in earnest.

A favorite of creative types like us is **oxymoron** or **paradox**, those images that, by their very contradictory essense, stick in the mind. The paradigm of this, of course, is John Milton's description of what Satan plunges through when cast out of Heaven to Hell: "darkness visible." Still, you can find examples in your daily life: "fabulously boring," "deafeningly silent," "gloriously stupid." One of my favorites comes from the old Eagles' song "Hotel California": "She was terminally pretty."

Far more frequently than these specific figures of speech, writers employ **metaphorical language**, which attributes charactertistics of one thing to something else, though the latter does not and cannot literally possess those qualities. If you turn to your nine-year-old who has just made a smart remark and say, "Button up," you tell him not to fasten his jeans but to shut his mouth. If you say, "the express train rocketed by," you essentially express the metaphor "the train was a rocket." Though obviously not literally the case, this gets across the idea that the train moves at a great rate of speed.

PROBLEMS WITH METAPHORS

For creative writers—well, perhaps for all writers—the major problems that arise with relation to metaphor involve inappropriate analogies, mixed metaphors, or cliché. The first of these—**inappropriate analogy**—is relatively easy to spot. As previously mentioned, metaphors within a piece should be in sync with the time, the place, and the characters the writer presents. Hence, for example, "General Washington's army came down upon the British like a bulldozer" might give the reader pause. In the Eighteenth Century there weren't any bulldozers, so the analogy—even if broadly accurate—is inappropriate. This can come up, too, simply in terms of tone. I read a story in which a character had eyes that were "Tidy-Bowl blue." This is surely a striking image, but the woman so described is a true object of the protagonist's desire. Readers get confused. They are supposed to believe that this young lady is beautiful, yet drawing a parallel between the color of her eyes and that of a toilet cleanser militates strongly against that idea. Obviously, if that writer's intent was to be ironic or comedic, then the description is perfectly apt. In this case, though, it violated the tone of the moment in the story.

Mixed metaphors can be a little trickier to spot and to use to attempt some sort of ironic or oxymoronic effect. A mixed metaphor presents two images so deeply in conflict that they contradict each other.

In Rod's depths of depression, selfishness was paramount.

The problem here is that we have two words—*depth* and *depression*—that indicate something low, followed by a word—*paramount*—that implies height. The images run smack into each other and confuse the readers.

The mixed metaphor is often a sign that you're getting carried away with your figurative language. Just like any other kind of description, parallels and analogies can be overdone to the point that the audience has so many competing pictures in its head that none has any real impact. The readers, to coin a phrase, "can't see the forest for the trees."

Which brings us to clichés.

We all know a **cliché** when we see one—or we think we do. English, like all other languages, abounds with hackneyed expressions that are so predictable as to be meaningless: "pretty as a picture," "right as rain," "ugly as sin," "cry like a baby." Well, you get the idea.

The word *cliché* itself comes (as you probably guessed) from French and is remarkably new. It literally means "stereotype" and refers to a process of casting a metal plate to be used for reproduction of a text, a picture, and so on. Clichés are, ironically, largely the victims of their own success. The reason that saying something such as "The basement room was bright as day" sounds old hat is that the image itself is so right. That's one well-illuminated cellar! However, the expression has been used hundreds of times before to describe the quality of brightness, so, consequently, its capacity to make an impression on our imaginations is virtually nil.

The origins of clichés vary. A lot of these expressions were once fresh and original. The King James Version of the Bible has given us, among others, "the four corners of the earth" (from Isaiah) and "O, ye of little faith" (from Matthew). Shakespeare provided in a single passage of *Romeo and Juliet* both "what's in a name" and "a rose by any other name would smell as sweet." Samuel Taylor Coledridge's Ancient Mariner first found an albatross around his neck, while Robert Burns mused about "the best-laid plans of mice and men." It is not merely the famous who originate clichés. Somebody named Samuel Smiles, in what sounds like a thrilling tome about Victorian virtue, *Thrift*, came up with "a place for everything, and everything in its place." Sometimes, clichés are themselves deformations of quotations from literary works. We assert that "music has charms to sooth the savage beast," though, when William Congreve coined the phrase in *The Mourning Bride*, he was concerned with music's capacity to sooth "the savage breast."

Other clichés can be traced to newspaper columns, political speeches, sermons, almanacs, fables, and jokes. Some simply have been around so long we don't really know where they came from. These adages, old sayings, morals of the story have simply taken up residence in our collective imagination and will probably be there indefinitely. In everyday life clichés can be useful to us, providing ready-made responses to a variety of circumstances in which, quite frankly, we may not have the time or want to take the trouble to respond to more orginally.

In writing, however, the situation is different. With all clichés, the general rule is simple: Avoid them. I recently read a story that, from the very first paragraph, promised to be a virtual epitome of hackneyed prose. After the protagonist had suffered many "trials and tribulations," things had finally "gone his way," so that his friends were "singing a different tune" and he was approaching the point where he would see his "dreams come true."

The prose got a shade more original after that, but reading the piece was (ahem) pretty rough sledding. The author continued to pepper his work with expressions that the reader can fill in after having read the first word.

However (didn't you just know this was coming?), there are ways this story or one like it might have worked. As with many other rules in writing, that banning clichés is not absolute when the work in question is creative. One way for cliché to be useful is as a means of characterization. Indeed, this is not uncommon. Readers don't need to be told that a character who constantly speaks in commonplaces isn't the most imaginative gal around. The writer can signal a character's limitations by having her constantly employ the stereo-typical in her descriptions, exclamations, and so on. Had the author of the piece we just mentioned been employing cliché in this fashion, the story might well have demanded an ironic or satirical reading, and so would have succeeded.

Further, just like real people, characters may use clichéd expressions when they're bored, inattentive, or detached from a conversation or circumstance. In my novel *The Book of Marvels*, the first words out of my protagonist's mouth are "That's a fact, Momma. Hotter than the blue blazes. It is." Pretty conventional stuff. However, as the story begins, Lila Mae is a pretty conven-tional woman, narrow in her vision of the world and its possibilities. The overarching point of the book is to show her growth. Beyond this, on that first page, Lila Mae is painting her nails as she talks on the phone with her domineering mother, who pesters her constantly. Her thoughts during the conversation center on her new nail polish—she's concluded she really doesn't like it. Her mind is not focused particularly on the heat, her mother, or her metaphors. It's not surprising, then, that she should fall back on overused, practically meaningless phrases.

Also, in the right circumstances, cliché lends itself to irony. Let's say you have a character who's convinced his very urban girlfriend to accompany him on a camping trip at a nearby lake. If her first words as she steps from the car and takes in the scene are "By the shores of Gitche Gumee, By the shining big sea waters," readers will not think she's a Longfellow fan or that she's falling back on *Hiawatha* because she can't think of anything more original to say. Rather, they'll know she's expressing her disaffection with this entire little project.

Cliché can imply an ironic or sarcastic distance, a kind of bored understatement. Here a character who's always in the midst of some personal drama and shows up in yet another stew on his neighbor's doorstep:

> "God, Fred, I'm so sorry. But it's really bad. I've gotta talk to somebody!"
>
> Fred looked up from the book he was reading and eyed Larry, framed by the screen door. Fred sighed. "Go ahead. Make my day."

Fred does not believe that Larry's really in trouble or has a true crisis on his hands. Rather, Fred expects that, once again, his neighbor is blowing some minor problem out of proportion. The allusion to Clint Eastwood's famous line as Dirty Harry in *Sudden Impact* is an indication of Fred's resignation before Larry's ongoing theatrics, and perhaps, given that the actor utters the line while holding a loaded gun, a veiled threat.

Cliché is subject to history. For the next decade or so, at least, the expression "I feel your pain" will be a no-no thanks to President Clinton and the comics and satirists who picked up on his frequent use of this phrase and had a field day with it. However, by 2020 or 2040, the general memory of this may have faded. A student in one of my introductory writing classes had a character say, "I want to be alone." In the margin, I immediately noted that these words were so intimately associated with Greta Garbo that, in a film made late in her career, *Ninotchka*, she and other characters actually parody her use of it. When the class met, however, all but three students—a film studies major and two people in their fifties—were perplexed by my objection. For the rest of the group, largely in their twenties, *Ninotchka*, Garbo, and "I vant to be alone" were simply unknown. The actress and her most famous phrase are, apparently, fading from the collective memory, so the phrase may, within a short time, once again be employed without the stigma of cliché.

Certain expressions are subject to changes in daily life and in technology. Consider the commonplace "like a broken record," as in "She went on complaining like a broken record" or "Bobby was so excited about the circus, he sounded like a broken record." Most people probably still know what this means: "repetitiousness like that produced by a scratched or otherwise damaged phonographic recording disk which skips the needle back to the same point on the surface again and again." However, an entire generation has never used (and perhaps never even seen) a phonograph nor "put on," "played" or "changed" a "record." They have lived in a world of CDs, DVDs, minidisks, and so on. It is possible that in thirty years this particular cliché will have vanished from the language because the technology which gave rise to it has disappeared.

In sum, the thing to remember—and this isn't surprising—is that the use of cliché in your writing is fine as long as it's appropriate and you're conscious of why that is the case. This is one reason why rereading, revising, and editing are so important. All of us, in the rush of creation, fall back on stock phrases in description and dialogue because we're anxious to move our stories forward. Had the cliché-ridden piece mentioned before ("trials and tribulations," "dreams come true," and so on) been merely a first draft, it would have been fine. However, the author didn't go back and consider, line by line, what he had written. Had he done so, he (I hope) would have recognized his overuse of commonplaces and changed them.

14

New Words

Language changes all the time, altered by new developments in technology, by interactions among different cultures, by changes in the way people live. Writers themselves change language by inventing words and expressions that more accurately or elegantly say what is intended. Forty years ago, if someone had talked about having to "download" some information, nobody would have had the vaguest notion of what he was talking about. If, eighty years ago, someone had made a remark, thought better of it, and said, "Hold on. Rewind," they'd have probably carted her off to the nearest nuthouse.

These terms, of course, derive from computers and tape recorders, which are now part of daily life. Indeed, the latter may even be on its way out as a quotidian fixture. It's entirely possible that, in fifteen more years, most people will find *rewind* as anachronistic as the verbs *gee* ("to turn to the right") and *haw* ("go left"), both common in a time when a lot of folk moved around on horseback.

Whereas equestrians are familiar with this terminology, the vast majority of us aren't. Back in the distant past, however, these terms were themselves probably **neologisms**, literally "new words" that were invented to deal with new developments in human living.

JARGON

Many neologisms begin life as **jargon** or **argot**, specialized language employed by a select few who are engaged in a similar activity or are familiar with a particular technology or set of ideas. When in an odd or frightening situation we commonly say we are "getting paranoid," but your great-great-grandparents would have had, at best, only a foggy notion of what that signified. *Paranoia* was once a clinical word whose use would have been confined to those involved in the relatively young science of psychology. Likewise, during World War II—when, in the midst of a general mobilization, almost everyone had some relationship to the military— learned a whole generation of words and expressions that related to that particular world: *spit shined* for "well polished," *head* for "bathroom," *snafu* ("*situation normal, all—ahem—fouled up*) for "an error."

The space race gave us such nifty expressions for getting angry as "go ballistic" and "send into orbit." Radio communications provided *roger* for "understood" and *out* for "good-bye." Until we had basketball, nobody's success was a "slam dunk;" and until baseball came along, no young swain dreamed of "getting to first base" or beyond with his date on Saturday night.

Over time, some words of this sort enter into the common parlance; some don't. Some slip into the language and subsequently fall out, just like slang does (see chapter fifteen). "Highball" may to some people still be familiar as a drink made with whiskey and soda, but it is also a verb meaning "to go ahead, particularly at a high rate of speed." This came from railroad signals, where a large ball would be raised on a tower adjacent to the tracks to indicate that a train could proceed without problems. Your father's father would have had no trouble comprehending "We got our stuff and highballed it out of there," whereas you might well be mystified.

A similar phenomenon has occurred frequently with brand names: We say "band-aid" for bandage, "kleenex" for tissue, and "xerox" for photocopy. Ironically, though, those who make these products often see this as an annoying development. After all, these are registered trademarks. Still, there isn't much they can do to change the situation. About their only hope—if that's the right word—is that their products will become *less* popular. There was a time, after all, when *Victrola* meant any record player, and *Kodak* was a generic term for camera. Obviously, things have changed.

BORROW WORDS

In addition, there are, of course, **borrow words**. This literally means what it says: Words from one language are imported to another to fulfill a particular function. What gets borrowed can vary greatly, even within a single language. In most of Latin America, for example, the English *computer* was simply Hispanicized as the word *computadora*, whereas, in Spain—which has a Royal Academy to keep an eye on things—the official word for your average Toshiba or MacIntosh is *organizador*. The French Academy constantly fights a desperate rearguard action against barbarbic invaders, particularly those from across the channel or the ocean. However, English—bastard tongue that it is—has always borrowed with great abandon. We commonly employ words drawn not only from the obvious candidates—Greek, Latin, German, and French—but from Dutch (*hodgepodge*), Russian (*apparatchik*), Hindi (*thug*), Italian (*bravura*), Arabic (*mufti*), Japanese (*futon*), Yiddish (*chutzpah*), Mandingo (*mumbo jumbo*) and Bantu (*goober*), to name just a few. Even the word *hoosegow* ("jail") which seems like a quintessential Americanism, comes originally from the Spanish *juzgado* ("tribunal").

We noted, when we discussed the use of accent marks (chapter nine in Part I), that words imported from other languages usually begin their English lives with their foreign spellings intact. Hence, we write "mise-en-scène," "coup de grâce," "soupçon," and so on. Over time, however, as these words enter into common English usage, the accent marks tend to fall away. This is more often the case with common nouns than proper nouns, which are oftentimes somebody's name. We still render the umlaut for German artist Albrect Dürer and the acute accent for Spanish poet Federico García Lorca. This is less true with place names, which, in any case, we often deform, altering the spellings entirely: Firenze has become Florence; São Paulo, Sao Paolo; Córdoba, Cordova.

With common nouns, these deformations are much more frequent. "Façade" appears more and more frequently as "facade" (even though somebody unfamiliar with the word might pronounce it "fah-kaid"). Many people now refer to fine wool from the Andean *vicuña* (vee-coo-nya) as "vicuna" (veye-coo-nah), and we have domesticated the pronunciation of the name of this animal's larger cousin, the *llama*, from yah-mah) into lah-mah. Though ordering an individual item off a menu is, properly speaking, asking for something "à la carte," it is often written "a la carte."

Borrow words may come and go. Huck Finn employs the Norwegian *flinders* to mean "splinters" or "pieces," which indicates it must have been a common enough term around Missouri in the mid Nineteeth Century—a period when there was a notable increase in Scandanavian immigration into the plains states. Nowadays, of course, that word strikes us as odd, at best. With the continued growth of the Latino population in the United States, it is probably safe to assume that Ricky Martin's "la vida loca" will remain a fixture in the language, though, given the fate of the lambada (does anyone remember that dance step?), perhaps we shouldn't be too sure.

COINAGE

Finally, writers—not just poets and novelists, but journalists and politicians—now and then invent words or phrases, which is referred to as **coinage**. Shakespeare was a past master of this. No one before his time had ever experienced "amazement" or had anything "uncurled." He gave us the word *epileptic*, along with *slugabed*. Before his plays appeared on the boards, nobody had ever been the victim of "foul play" in the sense of murder, nor had anything "beggared description" or "vanished into thin air." Shakespeare was the first to have someone find himself "in a pickle," living his "salad days," or serving as a "tower of strength."

Authors didn't stop inventing words and expressions after the English Renaissance. The first time somebody "chortled" (a cross between a "chuckle" and a "snort") was in Lewis Carroll's *Through the Looking-Glass*, while Joseph Heller provided the "catch-22." Interestingly, his novel was originally called *Catch 18*, but editors thought that might lead to its confusion with a recent best-seller, *Mila 18* by Leon Uris, the author of *Exodus*. Hence, our quintessential expression for circumstances of maddening frustration in which the very rules that govern the problem or situation seem to prevent any kind of solution was the result of a lunchtime confabulation between the author and representatives of his publishing house.

If the Twentieth Century owed the reality of the Iron Curtain to Joseph Stalin, it owed the expression to Winston Churchill, and Warren G. Harding (or one of his speechwriters) supposedly invented the term *normalcy* to mean "normality." In strictly linguistic terms, there was no such thing as a "masochist," at least in English, until 1893, when the twenty-first edition of *Dunglison's Medical Dictionary* included the term, derived from the name of Leopold von Sacher-Masoch, an Austrian novelist who had quite vividly depicted this particular sexual predilection in novels such as *Venus in Furs*.

Some really striking coinages never quite make the grade. The surrealist poet George Barker, for example, invented to describe the horrors of modern warfare he observed in the Spanish Civil War the word *calamiterror*, which seems about as apt a characterization as any other I've heard. In my novel *Mrs. Randall*, I tried to sneak into English the word *insolite*—derived from the lovely Spanish word *insólito* meaning "unusual" or "distinctive"—though I haven't noticed it being used in the last fifteen years. The same is true with my other stab at coinage: the term *thanateros* for "love-death" (though maybe this somewhat pretentious Latinism hasn't caught on because Richard Wagner had already invented, in *Tristan und Isolde*, the word *liebenstod*, which means the same thing.)

SO, WHAT DO YOU DO?

In keeping with this book's theme, your use of these kinds of words depends largely on the audience you are writing for and what and whom you are writing about. A legal thriller will feature a certain amount of legalese; a police procedural, the specialized terminology that cops, district attorneys, and forensic pathologists use among themselves. Science fiction and fantasy almost inevitably involve the development of some kind of lexicon to characterize worlds that are decidedly distinctive from our own. Perhaps the most famous illustration of this is in Anthony Burgess's *A Clockwork Orange*, which even includes a glossary of words of the Anglo-Russian vocabulary the author has invented for his pathological protagonists.

Still, an overuse of specialized language can make a piece of work look hermetic and off-putting. There's been great negative criticism over many years of the language of contemporary literary criticism itself, for example, due to the popularity within the academy of various schools of philosophy, psychology, anthropology, and so on, which has led to the use of words such as *bricollage* and *reify* and *schizeme*. Who knows, maybe some of these will settle into the language in a couple of decades, and we won't give their presence a second thought.

Nonetheless, when you're tempted to employ obscure vocabulary or to invent a brand new word or expression, at least give it some thought before you plunge ahead. Will your reader be able to figure out what you mean because of either the context or the commonly known root, even if he's never seen the word before? You shouldn't have to constantly provide definitions of the terminology you employ. This is true even in scholarly writing, and even more so, obviously, in fiction or other creative work. Particularly with creative texts, readers probably don't want to feel they're attending a seminar on a new subject.

One strategy you can employ when using a word you fear your reader may

not be familiar with is to explain the word without stopping the action to
define it. This can be done narratively or in dialogue. Have a look at the
following examples:

> "Aye. You'll likely find him up at the tarn."
> The image of the glittering waters of the lake bubbled up from her
> memory. Of course. That was where Bryan would be, there on those
> banks with the bare and jagged peaks crowding all around him.
>
> ———
>
> "Does she really have to go with us?" Kelly whined and made a moue.
> "You can wipe that pout off your face," her mother warned. "Mandy's
> your cousin, and you owe her some sympathy!"

You can see how, in both these instances, the word (*tarn, moue*) that may
be unfamiliar to your reader is explicated ("a small mountain lake," "an expression of disappointment or disdain") without smacking him across the face.
Still, this is a technique to use sparingly. If you constantly have to clarify your
vocabulary, then you probably ought to use a different vocabulary.

15

Slang, Colloquialism, and Dialect

As individuals, we each have what is referred to as an **idiolect**, the peculiar and distinctive manner in which we speak. An idiolect includes a vocabulary, particular figures of speech, verbal crutches, and other quirks of expression, as well as the different **registers** used to communicate with others. Registers are the modes of expression we employ to talk to different groups or individuals we come in contact with. You don't speak to your mother in the same way you speak to your friends, just as you speak differently to the boss than to your co-workers. Testifying before a jury in court, you are likely to use a relatively formal and even unnatural diction that sounds competely different from how you would later recount your testimony to your buddies down at the Dew Drop Inn.

The way a person speaks is determined by a tremendous number of factors: her historical moment; her class, race, or ethnic background; her places of residence, past and present; her parents' places of residence; and her membership in certain subcultures are just a few examples. A friend of mine, a dyed-in-the-wool Midwesterner who moved his family to the South, found to his horror that his youngest son within a very short time pronounced *cute* as if it had three syllables and consistently responded to adults with *yus'ir* and *nom'um*." I suspect, though my friend may not have even noticed, that he himself was beginning to pick up certain Southern tics, particularly that immensely useful pronoun *y'all.* We acquire our manner of speech in part from those around us, and that manner is mutable—at least to a point—over our entire lives.

SLANG AND COLLOQUIALISMS

Many of our registers are marked by the use of certain **slang** or **colloquialisms**. To distinguish between these two terms, think of slang as "temporal" and colloquialisms as "geographical." Children in the 1990s were "rug rats" (slang); children in a hollow in Appalachia are "young'ns" (colloquialism). Slang comes and goes (and, on occasion, comes back again), while colloquialisms tend to have a longer shelf life, continuing from generation to generation. What was "swell" in 1923 was "cool" in 1956, was "boss" in 1969, and is "phat" today. However, New Yorkers still (colloquially) stand "on line" rather than "in line;" a neighboring farm in rural North Carolina remains "over yonder." A Bostonian vacationing in Florida soon learns that, in Pensacola, ordering a "coffee regular" means he'll get black coffee, not the coffee and milk that he would normally expect at that little diner near Fenway Park.

Still, remember that this distinction, if convenient, is not absolute. Slang and colloquialisms are essentially identical in that they (like jargon) characterize certain communities. These are two linguistic ways that those who share a particular characteristic—be it place of origin, particular interests, or even something so broad as age—identify themselves, each to the other. As such, words and expressions can add a great deal of authenticity and resonance to your writing.

Slang and colloquialisms in your prose depends, again, on whom you are writing about, when your story takes place, where it takes place, and whose company your characters are in from scene to scene. Let's say that protagonist Wallace (a.k.a. Wally) lives in the suburbs of Lawton, Oklahoma, in 1968. He's a senior in high school and is looking toward a date with his classmate Missy. Here he is with his buddies, Roger and Billy.

"Shit, man, I am so psyched! Y'all know what a fox Missy is! It's gonna be just bitchin'! No gnarly times for me, guys!"

Here he is with Missy, convincing her to go with him to a roadhouse across the state line in Texas.

"It's a groovy place. They're doing a land-office business every weekend, baby! Your folks need to know zip about it."

With Missy's father, Wally's diction changes again.

"Yes, sir. I'll have Missy back by midnight. Don't you worry your head about it, sir."

You can see the differences in these registers. With his friends, Wally is vulgar and slangy; with Missy, he employs slang as well, though he avoids terms she might find objectionable. However, with Missy's dad, he's intensely polite and uses no slang at all.

Even though he's in Lawton, he's drawing from a variety of sources for his slang. After all, he listens to Top 40 radio and tries to be as hip and cool as seventeen-year-old boys in New York or Miami or Santa Monica. "Gnarly" and (arguably) "bitchin' " are surfer slang from the West Coast; Jimi Hendrix has given him "fox" from "foxy," likely originally a piece of inner-city African-American lingo. Wally's is a language that, in the early days of really abundant and constant mass communication, partakes of sources from coast to coast.

He does, however, slip into a colloquial turn of speech, "worry your head," when talking to Missy's dad. In an even more specifically regional turn of phrase, he does this with Missy—"land-office business" has particular resonance in Oklahoma, the state which began with the famous (or infamous) Land Rush.

Note as well that, in at least some of Wally's slang, we are cued as to the time period in which the story is unfolding. "Psyched," "fox," "know zip"— these are all expressions from the 1960s and are still in relatively common use. "Groovy" and "bitchin'," however, despite fitful revivals, now seem notably dated and direct us back to a period thirty years ago.

The use of slang and colloquialism is fine if it's appropriate to your story, that is, a kind of language that your narrator or other characters logically would employ given age, historical moment, location, occupation, and so on. Such words can provide richness and authenticity, convincing the readers that your tale is unfolding in a real world imbued with those real, if passing, expressions that characterized the time. Beware that this kind of vocabulary has certain pitfalls. First of all, it can make your story hermetic, or limited in its audience appeal. As with jargon and its relatives, if your narrative or dialogue is so loaded with time- or place-related lingo that it requires an expert in the milieu to figure out what's going on, then, obviously, you freeze out a considerable number of readers.

Remember that this kind of language, especially slang, can make a story seem dated after a short time. Frankly, this is a tough call. A writer wants his piece to have immediacy and to honestly represent the way his characters speak (or spoke). At the same time, the writer doesn't want readers to scratch their heads as they try to figure out what on earth his characters are talking about. It's entirely possible to tell a tale of contemporary techno and leave most of readers entirely at sea, as would be the case in a narrative about coal miners in West Virginia in 1923. With slang and colloquialisms, you can create a text that's completely correct in its terminology and completely opaque to your audience.

One way to manage this is to consider how actors deal with regional accents. Years back, I saw an off-off-Broadway play that was set in Maine during the Great Depression. The first scene opened on two young people who were "ferning"—collecting from the bogs ferns to be sold to florists in Boston and New York. The actors had obviously worked very hard on their "down east" inflections—so hard, in fact, that they were completely unintelligible. The dialogue might as well have been in Lithuanian. They would have been far better off flattening some vowels here and there to sign their New Englandness.

In general, writers are pretty good at determining how much time- or place-centered language to use. The biggest problems here tend to arise when the author employs a dialect.

DIALECT

Broadly, **dialects** are modes of speech that are distinct from the standard or literary language employed and/or endorsed by the educated ruling class of a particular nation or region. In this general definition, *dialect* can subsume other linguistic distinctions—**pidgin**, for example, which is a hybrid language (one composed of elements of more than one language, such as combinations of English, French, Spanish, Native, and African tongues found among Caribbean populations), or the **vernacular**, which we use to mean "everyday language." (The vernacular, or "the vulgar tongue," was originally the tongue used by the bulk of a population as opposed to that used by their rulers. Anglo-Saxon, for example, was the vernacular in England after the Norman Conquest, where the victors at the Battle of Hastings spoke French and Latin.)

Dialects are themselves languages, and, though you may not be conscious of it, they adhere to their own rules. They have their own idiomatic expressions, their own vocabulary, their own means of forming words (their "morphology"), their own syntax, and their own sounds ("phonology"). Hence, that question of consistency in a character's mode of expression is an essential one. If, for example, you decide you want a speaker to pronounce the initial *th* as a *d,* as in "dat" for "that," remember she will also say "dese," "dose," and "dem" for "these," "those" and "them," though she will not say "doughtful" for "thoughtful" unless she has a really bad cold. This is because of the subtle difference in the way *th* is pronounced in "thoughtful" and "that," for example (try saying the two words aloud and feel where your tongue goes).

It's a common strategy to indicate dialect by employing variant spelling to sign dropped or elided sounds in speech, though this can get awfully complicated awfully fast. Dropped *gs* on present participles and gerunds, collapsed words ("Gimme that," "lotsa," "woulda," and the like), and other orthographic peculiarities (one I saw recently was "yule" for "you'll") can get old for the reader very quickly. Beyond that, altered spellings can tie the writer into knots. Recall that the goal is to provide the audience with the flavor of a character's voice, not a ten-course meal of absolutely accurate linguistic transcript. Do this without needlessly slowing the action or, even worse, forcing the audience to read and reread a passage in order to figure out what in the name of God it says.

It's often easier to indicate dialect by means of narrative detail and the kind of words, expressions, and images a character employs.

> "Pshaw! A boy like Billy don't have a sparrow's worth of sense when it comes to courting a pert young filly like Pammy!"
>
> ———
>
> "Why, Miss Beaumont," he drawled lazily, "I don't have a notion what you mean."

You can imply a lot about the setting, the historical period, and the relationships of the characters by the very words they use and the tone of their interactions. Look at the following exchange between father and son:

> "So, you done your chores, Bobby?"
> "Yes, sir."
> "And you asked your mama?"
> "Yes, sir."
> "I don't know, son. Ten o'clock's awful late for a boy to be out."
> "But, Pa! I'm sixteen. It's not fair."
> "That back talk, boy?"

"No, sir!"

"All right. Well . . . I reckon it's all right. Go on ahead. But you
better have that little tail of yours back here at ten on the button when
you said."

"I will, sir. I promise! Thank you, Pa. Thank you."

First of all, you'd likely predict that this snippet of dialogue did not occur
in 2002 in Beverly Hills. What's significant here is that, even without variant
spelling, readers can hear the exchange in voices with a twang or drawl. There
is something rural, old fashioned, Southern, or Western about the vocabulary
and the very way this father and son interact. "You done," "chores," "your
mama," "Pa," "boy," "back talk," "reckon," "go on ahead," "little tail of
yours," and so on, along with what is now the exaggerated deference of son
to father, all create a particular impression of these characters and encourage
readers to imagine them in particular ways.

The point is that the exchange evokes the feel of dialect without actually
trying to transpose the mode of speech directly onto the page. It employs certain
expressions and conventions we associate with particular regions or historical
periods to locate and establish these characters. Readers "know" Bobby and his
father, understand the relationship between the two of them, and comprehend
their interactions without the need for various orthographic weirdnesses. Remember that the point of your telling is that the readers grasp your characters and
their vision of the world, a reaction that bears them along even if that vision is
entirely contrary to their own. Your greatest success comes when the nice Jewish
girl from Nassau County in Long Island can read the dialogue between a Tennessee father and son and know exactly the mentality and social reality that infuse
the dialogue and let her, at seventeen, see into a world she does not know but
can understand viscerally by the way you present it.

What strikes me as a slavish attempt to re-create a particular regional accent
that, despite the popularity of the story at the time it was written, ultimately
hobbles the impact of the tale can be found in Thomas Wolfe's "Only the
Dead Know Brooklyn." Have a look at the narrator's remarks on how he
learned to swim:

"Well, it's easy," I says. "All yuh need is a little confidence. Duh way
I loined, my older bruddeh pitched me off duh dock one day when I

was eight yeahs old, cloes and all. [. . .] When yuh know yuh got to, you'll do it. Duh only t'ing yuh need is confidence. An' once yuh loined," I says, "you've got nuttin' else to worry about. You'll neveh forget it. It's sump'n dat stays wit yeh as long as yuh live."

On one hand, Wolfe himself, a young man from the hills of Carolina, was surely fascinated by this urban English so different from that he had learned in a Southern resort town and later at the University of North Carolina and Harvard. There's something brave in his attempt to capture its flavor. At the same time, there are points here where we almost want to go "Okay, okay! We get it!" After all, don't most of us pronounce "clothes" as "cloes"? Further, is Wolfe entirely consistent in his variants? Would the Brooklyner who says "yuh loined" say "you've got" rather than "yuh got?"

When you are tempted to write overtly in dialect, consider that your choosing to do so implies you actually know the dialect and understand how it works (which can be two very different things). It further obligates you to be consistent in its usage throughout your text. Mark Twain was proud enough of his mastery of dialects in *Huckleberry Finn* to draw the readers' attention to this matter in an "Explanatory" at the beginning of the book:

> In this book a number of dialects are used, to wit: the Missouri Negro dialect; the extremest form of the backwoods Southwestern dialect; the ordinary "Pike County" dialect, and four modifed varieties of the last. The shadings have not been done in a haphazard fashion, or by guesswork; but painstakingly, and with the trustworthy guidance and support of personal familiarity with these several forms of speech.

As a riverboat pilot, Twain had heard and really listened to the variant Englishes that existed along the Mississippi. His book is the richer for their presence, though we might argue that, especially nowadays, it is the rare reader who actually picks up on the differences in speech that Twain employed with, say, the Grangerford family and the Duke and the Dauphin.

I confronted a minor instance of this in a student novel in which contemporary characters in their early twenties frequently employ the locution "aw right." Schoolmarmishly, perhaps, I corrected these to "all right." The author, in reponse, wrote me a note indicating she, of course, knew the proper spelling of *all right*, but arguing that, in fact, *aw right* possesses in twenty-first-century lingo a slightly different valence than the traditional expression does.

I'm certainly willing to buy that argument. Indeed, it was expressed quite eloquently by the writer. I did suggest to her, however, that she should be prepared to make the same case to agents, editors, and copyeditors along the way. The notion that the expression with a variant spelling constitutes an element of the slang or dialect of the characters is perfectly legitimate. However, publishers are generally inclined to adhere to conventional forms unless the writer can justify breaking them.

Again, it's your call. As regards the issues discussed here and in other chapters, find some sort of via media in which the richness and distinctiveness of your characters' language come across without making the characters unintelligible.

16

Offensive Words

Words that people find offensive generally fall into two categories: **derogatory and blasphemous** or **obscene**. The former category, frankly, has grown larger and larger over the last few decades, whereas the latter has shrunk. *Greaser* or *queer* were terms most anybody knew and a great many people used in the 1950s without a second thought. Conversely, a word such as *butt* in that same decade would have been viewed if not precisely as obscene, then as a vulgar term inappropriate for use in mixed company.

Times have changed. You can hear *butt* used casually on television and can see *butt* (well, the word itself anyway) on billboards along the freeway. However, in our politically correct world, deprecatory terminology that pertains to individuals or groups has become unacceptable. For writers, this issue can get quite complicated. Many times in workshops tempers have flared and feelings have been hurt by textual language that, in contemporary usage, has been condemned to our lexicological "index prohibitorum." *Bitch, camel-jockey, canuck, chink, cracker, dago, faggot, frog, gook, honkie, Jap, JAP, kike, kraut, lesbo, mick, nigger, pansy, Polack, peckerwood, redskin, sheeny, slant, spic, spook, squaw, trailer trash, wog, wop*—English does not lack for dismissive terms for those who are perceived as "other" because of race, ethnicity, gender, sexuality, or economic class. Nowadays, in daily life, the terms retailed above can constitute fighting words, and—for most of us at least—they are simply unacceptable in everyday discourse.

The fact remains, like it or not, that these words are used, have been used, and will continue to be used by a great many people from sea to shining sea. Given this, the presence of these terms in our stories, whether fiction or nonfiction, is a given. For you as writer, employing them can be discomfiting;

on the other hand a degree of discomfort on the part of your audience may well be the point. This kind of terminology is inevitably an element of characterization of both individuals and the worlds they inhabit. Readers make certain assumptions about someone who says, "There are just too many slants downtown anymore," or "Stop acting like such a fag."

What's perhaps most problematic for a writer is the use of offensive words by characters who are intended to be sympathetic. In the case of a thoroughly villainous figure, we have few qualms about peppering his speech or thoughts with blatantly obnoxious verbiage—this merely emphasizes his narrowness or wickedness. The racist rantings of Faulkner's Percy Grimm may make us cringe, but that's precisely the intent. These characters are supposed to be repellent, and their voicing of ugly prejudices simply adds to their gruesome personalities.

We shy away from this kind of language when creating a protagonist, but, in the end, the character becomes inappropriate or unrealistic. The simple, unfortunate truth is that ours remains a culture that is racist, sexist, homophobic, and so on, and even the most sensitive and progressive among us, despite our best efforts to the contrary, have consciousnesses cluttered with expressions and terminology and even ideas that, intellectually, we find are anathemas. And surely, all our characters are not merely our personas, our own selves transposed on the page. As writers, we can create individuals who, though good and admirable, are not as thoughtful as we may be when it comes to dealing with or talking about those who belong to "other" groups. Further, if we deal with incidents and individuals in a time thirty or eighty or three hundred years ago, we must use many words and notions, that far from being viewed as noxious, were widely shared and socially endorsed.

For example, I recently read an apprentice novel that is set up as a series of monologues by various characters inhabiting an economically depressed neighborhood downriver from Detroit. The story is set in the early 1970s, and the central figure in the story is a thirtyish white man who runs a diner in the neighborhood. For a number of reasons, he is not entirely typical of those around him, having been away from the area during his service in the army and, perhaps more important, having come into ownership of his restaurant as a kind of front man for its African-American owner. Still, it is clear in the story that the main character is very much the product of his seriously

dysfunctional upbringing, his marginal economic background, and the historical moment when the tale unfolds.

In reading the manuscript, I was struck by the fact that the character never
employed the notorious "n word" in reference to African-Americans, a fact
that, in the end, seemed to me unrealistic, given who he is purported to be.
In discussing this with the author, it emerged, of course, that he himself avoids
offensive language. Author and character, however, are not the same person.
The former long left behind his depressed childhood neighborhood; traveled
the country; earned a college degree; and over the years, encountered numerous
black friends, co-workers, and acquaintances. This is not the case, however,
with his protagonist, and the avoidance of the offensive term, especially in
relation to a young black employee with whom the protagonist has a vexed
relationship, seemed natural. Indeed, it actually undermined a powerful element in the plot. The protagonist, diagnosed with terminal cancer, ultimately
concludes that the young black man is the one most likely to sustain the
business he has helped build, and embraces him almost as a son.

The fact that the word *nigger* was avoided in the text undermined the
impact of what is obviously the story's emotional nexus. The author wants to
show us his protagonist's growth, his final transcendence of the traditions and
prejudices of his upbringing. However, if we have the sense that he has always
demonstrated toward African-Americans a certain sensitivity that we might
not expect of someone like him, his journey toward acceptance strikes the
reader as less significant than the author intends. The social commentary the
novel makes with regard to racism in American society loses some of its punch
due to the writer's own reluctance to employ language he disapproves of.

Offensiveness itself is not a fixed quality, but one subject to the ebb and
flow of the historical tide. The editor of my novel *The Professor of Aesthetics*
was concerned by a character's remark that the protagonist wouldn't "have
had a Chinaman's chance." There's no question that the accepted term today
for someone from China is *Chinese*. Still, that particular idiomatic expression
is one I can remember from my boyhood in Oklahoma, and there's little
question that it was part of the common parlance in 1932, when my character
employed it. It struck me as precisely what Justus Beckner would say at that
juncture. Short of excising it entirely, there seemed little way around using
what, in a contemporary context, would be deemed a racial slur, even though,

in the decade of the Great Depression, *Chinaman* would not necessarily have been viewed as demeaning.

Interestingly enough, the preferred term for those descended from Chinese, Korean, Japanese, Vietnamese and other Far Eastern roots is now *Asian* rather than the formerly accepted term, *Oriental*—this despite the fact that the former is so vastly general as to be almost meaningless. Turks, after all, unless they reside on the western side of the Bosphorus and the Dardanelles, are Asians, as are Israelis, Sri Lankans, Bangladeshis, Iranians, Azeris, Tanjiks, and anyone born in Vladivostok. Tunisians, Boers, Ugandans, and Nigerians are "Africans," yet it would seem absurd to use that term in any but the broadest context. Even the use of *American* for residents of the United States of America is, strictly speaking, problematic, in that Argentines, Canadians, Inuits, and anyone else who inhabits the Western Hemisphere is "American."

Polite terminology changes over time. *Colored* was, for many years, the preferred term for African-Americans, and it remains enshrined in the name of the oldest civil rights organization, the NAACP (National Association for the Advancement of Colored People). This designation was displaced in public parlance in the 1950s by *Negro*, which itself was superceded by *black*. In the United States, that word is probably in the process of being replaced by *African-American*. *Chicano* as a term for Mexican-Americans began life as a derogation. In the 1960s, it was adopted by more radical Mexican-American organizations, and it gradually found its way into accepted usage.

Related phenomena occur among other minority populations. The name of the rap group N.W.A., for example, stands for "Niggaz With Attitude," while, in the late 1980s, an activist gay organzation called itself "Queer Nation" and another group dubbed itself the "Radical Fairies." Various lesbian motorcycle clubs christened themselves "Dykes on Bikes," and white suburban teenagers who adopted the fashions and musical styles of blacks of the inner city proudly called themselves "wiggers." Not infrequently, words that would be considered inappropriate if used by outsiders are freely employed within a minority itself, sometimes almost as endearments. Hence, Bob Miklauski may say to his fellow Rotarian Jack Kywsinski, "Oh, come on, you dumb Polack" without a second thought, whereas he would never think of calling Joe Castiglione a "dumb wop."

It is worth recalling as well that some words in common use were initially racial or ethnic slurs. *Welsh* or *welch* (as in "renege, to 'welch' out on the deal") supposedly derives from English derogation of the honesty of the inhabitants of Wales. *Gyp*, as in "to cheat," comes from *Gypsy*. One hundred years ago, "to jew down" in the sense of "to bargain" was a relatively widespread expression, and *scotch* and *dutch* indicated a person was not simply "thrifty" but "cheap."

As in most instances, what is most significant in a work of the imagination is the accuracy of the use of such terms; that is, is this the word this character would employ? Huck Finn calls the escaped slave with whom he travels "Nigger Jim" not because Mark Twain wished to offend his audience or because he and his protagonist held Jim in contempt, but because that is the word a fourteen-year-old white orphan from Hannibal, Missouri, would have used in the mid Nineteenth Century. In a story set in 1784 a man sexually attracted to other men would not be "gay" or even "homosexual" but a "nance" or a "molly" or a "bugger" or a "sodomite"—in 1784, *homosexual* had not yet been invented, and *gay* did not yet have its present-day meaning.

As has been said again and again, don't overdo it. A word in print has greater impact than a word uttered. Beyond that, dirty words or sexist discourse, for example, should have some larger significance within the story itself and tell the readers something about the people they're dealing with. Avoid merely placing these on the page for shock value. Though opinions may differ, nine times out of ten it is easy to distinguish between the use of obscene or insulting language as a legitimate literary tool and its use as merely a gratuitous opportunity to express whatever ugly prejudices the author may harbor.

Pretty much all we have said with regard to offensive terminology that is racist, sexist, and so on is applicable to language that is offensive because it is blasphemous or obscene. "Talking dirty" has become almost the norm, but this is a relatively recent development, at least within the larger culture. It is not, certainly, that people did not swear in the Seventeenth Century or during the Civil War, but the use of such language was considerably more circumscribed than it is today. Women—at least those of or aspiring to a certain class status—did not curse at all, and while men did, their use of strong terms was limited to particular venues (the workplace, the tavern, the brothel). Other than in privately printed pornographic texts, many words we now hear on a daily basis were simply prohibited from appearing in print. Only after the middle of the Twentieth Century was this taboo broken.

This doesn't mean that many of our common swear words didn't exist.

A quick look at J.S. Farmer and W.E. Henley's *Slang and Its Analogues*, published in seven volumes between 1890 and 1904, reveals that our great-great-grandfathers would have known the meanings of *cock* or *muff* or *screw*. A large number of these words are far more ancient, as a perusal of the works of writers such as Ben Jonson or Geoffrey Chaucer reveal.

All languages have their dirty words, which often are manifestations of some particular concern or obsession of the culture that employs them. In Latin-based languages, many insulting terms pertain not directly to an individual but to the individual's mother, which reveals a great deal about how these societies view both motherhood and women in general. German insults, on the other hand, often relate to bodily functions and cleanliness, as might be expected in a people noted for their concern with neatness and order.

As you might predict, English is an "equal opportunity insulter," drawing its vulgar language from bodily functions ("a shitty engineer"), sexual activity ("go fuck yourself"), variant sexuality ("cocksucker"), motherhood ("son of a bitch"), and so on. Speakers of English have a peculiarly rich obscene vocabulary, as anyone who has attempted to translate a rough or racy text into a foreign language knows. Among other reasons, this may be because we lack common "polite" words for things that people, whether we like it or not, do everyday. Such terminology that does exist is often either clinical ("anal intercourse"), Latinate ("cunnilingus"), or overtly foreign ("fellatrice"). Aside from juvenile euphemisms such as "pee-pee" or "make dirt," we have no standard words for the acts of urination and defecation except those that are thought of as vulgar.

It's worth noting that Anglo-American culture has, for the last couple of centuries, taken a dimmer view of obscene words than blasphemous ones, despite the fact that, by the lights of the Judeo-Christian tradition, use of the latter is far more serious than that of the former. *Damn, hell, God, Jesus*— these are all equivalent to taking the Lord's name in vain, which violates the Third Commandment. Yet they appeared in print long before such words like *pussy* or *piss*, or even terms we now think of as merely vernacular rather than obscene, such as *ass* or *crap*. This is a reversal of the situation in Shakespeare's time, in which stage characters were freely allowed to say "turd in your teeth," but prohibited from blaspheming. It is in that era that we find the birth of what we think of now as amusing and archaic interjections like *zounds*, which was a means of avoiding the common expletive "God's wounds."

Where the use of such language is concerned, you need to ask yourself the same questions you do in relation to derogatory words: What function does this serve in my story? What does this reveal about my character and the world he lives in? Again, these terms have greater strength on the printed page than they do when they are spoken. In contemporary discourse, "fuckin" is often merely an intensifier, or a kind of time buyer in the course of a sentence. We simply don't hear it in the way we would read it. An old rule says you should write down a character's obscenity-laced speech just as you would hear it, then go back and cut out half of the dirty words.

You are not required to use words you or others may find offensive. Such authors as the Bröntes or Henry James or F. Scott Fitzgerald got along just fine without them. In making such a choice, bear in mind who your target audience is. If you're crafting a story you see as destined for *Seventeen*, the vocabulary you employ will inevitably be different than that you would use if you were writing for *Playgirl*. If this kind of language makes you uncomfortable, you have to either overcome that discomfort or develop fictional strategies that allow you to avoid it. That may not be easy. If, for example, you write about the "gangsta" world of the inner city, capturing the casual vulgarity that characterizes it may be tricky. Nonetheless, writers managed to write about World War I and its horrific mud and gas and gore without actually reproducing the vocabulary the doughboys undoubtedly used in the trenches. The audiences of the time, of course, knew this, and it is perhaps tougher today to avoid raunchy talk simply because the contemporary reader—accustomed to this kind of language in print media, film, the Internet, and even television—anticipates a realism (or hyperrealism!) in dialogue that would have shocked our grandparents.

Be careful with euphemism, the "nicer" word we often employ in conversation to avoid a grittier term (e.g., *have sex* in place of *fuck*). If your gangsta is with his latest one-night stand, he might say, "Okay, baby, let's do it," but he's unlikely to say, "Let's make love."

Your willingness to employ offensive terms may have a significant impact upon your writing—both its form and its content. By avoiding large swatches of dialogue in a story set in rural 1950s Alabama, you may obviate the need for racist speech, but you will need to make sure the piece does not become overgrown with narrative. If you want to avoid vulgar language, a story about interactions among contemporary suburban teenagers may simply be impractical. Listen to some Limp Bizkit or any of a number of contemporary rap singers, and you'll soon realize that there are no longer any prohibited words. In the end, you decide whether you and the audience you are writing for can read and appreciate the need for these kinds of terms.

One final irony is something that affects us as writers, though we are powerless to do anything about it. Earlier, I discussed how certain minorities have co-opted terms meant to wound them, thus expropriating the words and, ultimately, robbing them of their power. The same phenomenon has occurred with obscene language. My father, a naval aviator during both World War II and the Korean War, was certainly familiar with every naughty, vulgar, crude English expression for the human body, its functions, and its activities. And yet, I believe I was sixteen years old before I ever heard him use anything stronger than what were, by that time, the relatively mild expletives *hell* and *damn*, even in those moments in extremis (slamming his thumb with a hammer, for example). This seems quaint, but nowadays, when no word is considered inappropriate, when no word is reserved for particularly intense or private interactions, then these words lose their magic, their capacity to shock. The corruscating fire of a "Damn you!" in a nineteenth-century novel and the horror that greeted the acid obscenities of Edward Albee's *Who's Afraid of Virginia Woolf?* when it played on Broadway in the early 1960s belong to history. Today, language's capacity to literally freeze us in our tracks has vanished.

This has its positive side, of course, but consider the roots of *blaspheme* (Greek for "evil speech"), *obscene* (Latin for "ill augered"), and even *profane* ("outside the temple," and hence, "unsacred"). Remember that when we use this kind of language, we call it "cursing" or "swearing," acts that, in their literal sense, carry with them notions of the eternal and the supernatural. There is no more terrible example of how the domestication—dare I say, degradation—of "bad words" has impoverished us all than those we heard in the reponses to the destruction of the World Trade Center towers in New York in September 2001. "My God!" "O, Lord!" "Jesus Christ!" "Shit!" "Oh! Fuck!"—all of these sputter on the audio- and videotapes of that ghastly morning. These were utterances of fear or terror or disbelief, but in a world where we are accustomed to hearing, "My God! What a lousy sandwich," or "Malt liquor really fucks me up," these words no longer slap us across the face as they once might have. In eliminating the concept of "inappropriate language," we have, inadvertantly, lost a language commensurate with our capacity for wonder or horror or awe.

17

Descriptions

In an advertisement for some laxative, an elderly woman ponders a jar of prunes and wonders despairingly: "Are two too few? Are five too many?"

The image of regularity (as the copywriters who deal with this kind of publicity like to put it) may not be perfect, but this woman's dilemma is one writers know with regard to description. The consequences of overdosing or underdosing—logorrhea on one hand and a constricted and constipated prose on the other—can be dire. Like other topics in this book, any "rules" about description (are two adjectives too few? are five too many?) can almost immediately be countered by an obvious exception. Gustave Flaubert thought three significant details were sufficient to establish a place or character in the reader's imagination, something that later writers such as James Joyce and John Barth obviously did not take to heart. The amount and quality of description is heavily determined by such factors as the style adopted in a particular piece, whether a reader would have at least some familiarity with a particular locale or circumstance, and who does the describing.

In American letters, very generally, there are two competing styles. One, deriving initially from Shakespeare and the King James Version of the Bible, is highly rhetorical, elaborately metaphorical and allusive, often Latinate, dense and detailed. You can see this from writers as different as Melville and Pynchon, as Faulkner and Kerouac. The second school is stripped down, streamlined, and rapid. It appears in the late Nineteenth Century in the work of authors such as Stephen Crane and found its great, twentieth-century champion in Hemingway. It has since manifested itself in works as different as hard-boiled detective novels and the stories of the so-called minimalists of the 1980s like Raymond Carver and Anne Beatty.

Often, a writer varies her style to suit the tale she has to tell. Further, many authors fall somewhere between these two stylistic extremes. You need look no farther than a figure such as F. Scott Fitzgerald to find an example. The point is that, if you are clicking along in a spare and sinewy prose, it can be distracting to the reader if you suddenly spend an entire paragraph rich with similes and brimming with modifiers describing a character's bedroom. Of course, such a strategy can be perfectly justifiable. Perhaps you want to shift to a more ornate prose to slow the action, or you need to draw attention to that bedroom because it will be a locus of the story's events or because its details reveal unanticipated elements of a character. As ever, the key here is your intent, your consciousness of your altering style toward a particular end.

Another factor affecting description decisions is how unusual or exotic the world or the characters of a text will be for the average reader. One reason Carver, for example, was able to pursue that extremely spare style that some called "Kmart realism" was that the realm of his stories was familiar to a large segment of his contemporary audience. The strip malls and subdivisions, the freeways and fast-food joints, the television programs and other detritus of popular culture—these were all known quantities to most Americans two decades ago.

Still, even a contemporary setting in a contemporary city may require thorough description. Most readers likely need less retailing of the charms or ugliness of New York or San Francisco than they do for Columbus, Ohio, or Omaha, Nebraska. Thanks to tourism and film and endless other texts, the first two cities evoke images in a reader's mind that the latter two, however distinctive they may be, do not. The need for such details and description increases even more if your story is taking place in Lahore or Lagos or La Plata—places some of your readers may have never heard of. Still it's worth noting that the amount of space dedicated to the physical decription of place has declined overall in books written in the last hundred years. Nineteenth- and early-twentieth-century novelists like Charles Dickens or Edith Wharton spent considerable time and effort evoking cities, neighborhoods, streets, rooms, and so on, simply because their readers' knowledge of physical realities in the slums of London's East End or the interiors of mansions in Newport, Rhode Island, was likely limited at best. With only paintings and line drawings to go on—no photographs, films, or television—this audience obligated authors to literally paint "word pictures" to conjure visual images of places.

You can see this same phenomenon in modern texts that are set, for example, in the past or the future. We all have a pretty good idea of what Washington, DC, looks like, but Gore Vidal in his novel *Lincoln* had to deal with a city in which the Capitol dome was only half finished, the Washington Monument was a jagged stub on which construction had been suspended, and Pennsylvania Avenue was largely commercial and residential, not a boulevard lined with neoclassical behemoths that now house the various branches and sub-branches of government.

Beyond that, this Washington was an armed camp. On occasion a mere river's width away from the enemy, the city crawled with troops, and soldiers were billeted throughout its neighborhoods. Far more than in today's age of "homeland security," this capital was one at war and often felt like one under siege.

Consequently, Vidal had to evoke that different city for us in a way an author dealing with the contemporary city does not. This is true for writers of not only historical novels, but those classified as science fiction and fantasy. Among the reasons these two genres tend more toward the novel than the story is that an author must communicate the multiple peculiarities that make the fictional world distinct from the one we know.

CHARACTER DESCRIPTIONS

Beyond style, setting, and period, other factors affect the descriptions in a particular text. Most obviously, there are the questions of who is telling the story, where that character resides, even what his occupation is. In a first-person or third-person-limited narrative, what gets described and how are largely determined by the personality of the character through whose eyes we witness the action. If she is a chatty, Southern, small-town grandmother, she is likely to give details of family; dress; gardens; food; and the manners, good or bad, of others. If, instead, the central character is a gruff and bitter young man of twenty-three, he is less likely to know, share, or care about such information. Elaborate descriptions painted with a diverse palette of allusions and images are more likely to come from an educated or artistic or well-traveled or sensitive character than from one who has an eighth-grade education and has never ventured farther than one hundred miles from home.

Even in a more traditional third-person narrative, a writer needs to show some sensitivity to where a story is set and who its protagonists are. In a tale about the barrios of Los Angeles, it will strike the readers as odd if the narration reveals that a sudden storm is "brutal as a nor'easter," because an allusion to New England weather will seem out of place. In a narrative about the racers on the stock car circuit in the Southeast, a "sunset worthy of Monet" or "a girl dressed all in fucshia" would sound peculiar. Again, maybe the Chicano protagonist was born in Boston and the racing team is made up entirely of Duke graduates. The readers just need to know!

WORKING WITH DESCRIPTIONS

With all this said, let's turn to some more concrete suggestions about how to handle descriptions. On the whole, description merely for description's sake isn't worth much, and it tends to clot up a story. Details the writer includes should reveal something about a character, advance the plot, or, ideally, do both. If, in the first paragraph, Rob is driving a brightly polished '57 Chevy in cherry condition with a spick-and-span interior, it's probably safe to assume he's a guy who's into cars. Similarly if his chariot of choice is a '99 Neon with assorted dings and mud-flecked fenders, the reader can figure cars are not high on Rob's list of priorities.

Know that if the writer chooses to include the make, model, and condition of Rob's car, the reader will assume that Rob's auto fetish, or lack thereof, somehow relates to the story. If this is not the case, "Rob got out of his car and walked up to Cindy's door" is sufficient. You can't tell your readers absolutely everything about a character, so whatever you do choose to reveal should have some significance in the action they will witness.

Another common but useful piece of advice is to keep details **active** rather than merely **observational**, and use ones that are "sensory" rather than merely **descriptive**. An example of observational details is

Linda had limp, white-blond hair she wore in a ponytail down to her shoulders.

While an active version is

Linda's hair, blond almost to white, fell in a limp ponytail to her shoulders.

The first sentence simply tells about the quality, color, and style of Linda's hair, as if somebody were describing this woman's image in a photograph. In the second example, however, the emphasis is far more on Linda's hair itself. It is actually doing something—falling.

Where sensory detail is concerned, recall that the human animal, unlike many other species, is incredibly dependent on his eyes. We most commonly communicate information about something by telling somebody else what it looks like. Consequently, images drawn from our other, less frequently used senses often have a greater impact on a reader. Concretely, this means describing how something—a room or person or landscape—smells or sounds or feels or tastes. An old but helpful exercise is to write a couple pages from the perspective of a blind person. You'll be surprised at how skillfully you can evoke a world without depending on vision.

Say that Mandy's on a Caribbean vacation and is off for her first foray onto the beach.

> Mandy stepped from the cabana into the salty air. The sun was incredibly bright as she watched the waves lap gently on the shore. The sand was white as sugar and seemed more finely grained than any other she had ever seen.

Now, compare that to

> Mandy stepped from the cabana. The sunlight dazzled her, and she could taste the salt in the air. She heard the gentle lap of the waves on the shore, and, beneath her feet, the sugar-white sand was like silk.

The first version is perfectly okay, but I argue that the second has a far stronger impact on the reader. Just how bright that sunlight is comes through in that magical verb *dazzled*. Further, Mandy's state of being half blinded is emphasized by the fact that she is thrown back on taste, hearing, and touch to comprehend the scene before her. She registers on her tongue the salt in the air, and our impression is that initially she can hear but not really see the waves. Certainly, the tactile "like silk" gives us a far more sensual notion of the sand than the visual and almost scientific characterization of it as "finely grained."

It's not necessary to do this all the time. If you make the text too rich in any kind of description, the experience for the reader can be like overdosing on chocolate. Still, a good sensory description obviates the need for bald observation. Consider the following:

Sara knew Lars had been drinking. She could smell whiskey on his breath as he teetered there on the threshold.

Given what follows it, is that first sentence necessary at all? The second one makes clear what Lars has been doing.

Sara could smell whiskey on Lars' breath as he teetered there on the threshold.

As noted when we discussed modifiers in chapter three, writers can get so carried away expounding on absolutely everything that the reader simply gets lost. In a badly overwritten text, everything seems to be of equal significance, and the audience can't identify what really needs their attention vs. what is merely trying to keep the action moving. As with many facets of your writing, you may need to describe settings or characters at considerable length in an initial draft because you yourself are just discovering them. Go ahead and spell out color, dimensions, furnishings, dress, height, weight, and so on. Write as much as you need to lock the image of Natalie's bedroom or Todd's girlfriend in your mind. However, in subsequent drafts, cast a baleful eye on all that detail. Does it really need to be there? Do readers need to know that those blue throw pillows on Natalie's bed really set off the gray duvet? Is it really significant that Brenda is five-one rather than five-two or five feet even? Believe me, I know it's often hard to cut these passages. A writer becomes accustomed to their presence in the text, and they are often well written. To overcome the urge to keep rather than cut, simply remind yourself that your first obligation is to keep your reader engaged with the text, and excessive verbiage is a sure way to undermine that engagement.

These days, frankly, a lot of apprentice writers don't do *enough* describing. As with many other writing issues, this may be a result of too much television and other electronic stimulation. The narrative models viewers are most exposed to are those of the police serial and the sitcom, where the settings as well as the physical appearances, gestures, and expressions of characters are right there on the screen for all the world to see.

You don't have to painstakingly write about every little detail about a place or person. You cannot render an image as completely with words as you can on film, and this is not a bad thing. Reading is a far more collaborative effort and active undertaking than watching a movie or a television program. The writer provides certain cues to the reader, and she fills in the rest. Two imaginations work in tandem to create the world that the writer wants to present.

> All dark oak and maroon, the room unnerved Alice. It seemed about as different from what you would anticipate of Martin as anything could possibly be.
>
> She plopped onto one of the sofas, the cushions so overstuffed she feared she would simply vanish. A clock ticked ominously somewhere, but she had no luck locating it in the gloom.
>
> "Alice! Darling!" Martin bounced through the door like a labrador puppy, all feet and enthusiasm. "I'm so glad you're here! How was the trip? It's such a dull ride, really." He flipped aside a brown lock that had strayed over his glasses. "But no matter! We must have tea."

This passage provides few but significant details. From these, you fill in a great many details on your own. From what we read, we envision Martin's house as large, old, and dark. It is intimidating for Alice, and even a bit sinister (those carnivorous cushions, that ticking clock). The house doesn't seem to fit its owner at all, something reinforced when Martin arrives with canine adorableness, yapping out his greetings. His hair is brown, relatively long, and apparently not skillfully styled. He wears glasses.

We don't know the precise diminsions of the room, whether there are bookshelves or art or both lining the walls, what Martin is wearing, or if he is tall or short, but your mind probably has already provided these elements. Your image may, in fact, match neither the author's nor mine nor anyone else's precisely, though all the images readers form from these details will be similar. That is the wonder of writing: From the imperfect signs that are words, readers can share an experience and a vision that is collective and yet quirkily individual, nuanced because of their particular stocks of images and their own imaginations.

18

Pace, Balance, and Transitions

PACE

Everyone has, in the midst of reading a piece of prose, had his engagement lag. Something isn't working. The author has begun to lose the reader. The explanations for this are legion, but one of the most common is that the "pace" of the story is somehow "off."

Pace is, of course, the speed at which the action proceeds, and it can vary within even a short piece of prose. The story may accelerate or decelerate, depending on what is happening. Determining when the pace is just right is remarkably difficult, and "just right" depends upon the tale, the author's chosen style, and so on. Too, the reader's judgment is subjective. Some find the lingering, complex sinuousness of Marcel Proust's prose in *Remembrance of Things Past* intoxicating, while others find it soporific. Still, we can discuss pace in general terms in order to be alert to moments in our stories that may need adjustment.

A work can move either too fast or too slow. The former most often arises when there is a paucity of narrative. This is another instance where other media may have had a baleful effect on written prose. I often encounter in apprentice work what I refer to as scenes of "talking heads," long passages of nothing but dialogue between two characters. The effect is a bit like sitting in one room while the television is on in the other. You hear the voices, but you can't see the people, their body language, their postures, where they are, and so on. Scenes like this flash by, and readers do not feel part of what they're reading.

If you note in your work that all the words on a page are enclosed in quotation marks, look hard at it to see if some kind of narrative interruption—

the inclusion of a gesture, for example—might slow things down to the benefit of the passage. Conversations in real life, after all, don't proceed at a constant speed. We pause for emphasis or out of reticence or to sip our coffee. As we talk, our expressions change, we change positions, and we move around. We rarely sit and talk and do nothing else. Including pauses and actions in the passage adds greater realism to the moment, slows it down, and sometimes highlights what is truly notable.

This can be overdone and have the opposite effect. If readers get too many interruptions in the midst of dialogue, they lose track of what the conversation is about and start to drown in the detail. The effect can be comical. I've read stories whose characters seem to have a finger in an electrical socket or ants in their pants or a series of distressing tics. They are in constant motion— standing up, sitting down, pacing, drumming their fingers—and every subtle shift in their expressions or body language is duly registered.

Narrative passages are even more prone to this kind of excess. As we noted in chapter seventeen, writers may tend to spend in a first draft too much time and space on details that are useful for themselves but not essential for the readers. Hence, the admonition about an entire page of dialogue also applies to pages of unbroken narrative. Generally, narrative reads more slowly than dialogue does. Surely, there are instances where unbroken exposition is perfectly justified, but this implies a more leisurely unfolding of the action.

Pace also is influenced by the length of sentences. Longer sentences, given their greater complexity, require careful attention and read more slowly than others. Short sentences read fast. So, at points of climax, for example, you may want to employ more periods than commas and semicolons. At these presumably exciting moments, you aim for your reader to get caught up in them, to want to read faster, and to be able to do so.

The same holds for paragraphing. If appropriate to the writer's style, a paragraph that goes on for pages is perfectly plausible, but this is unusual. All that crowded print can put the brakes on a good read. If a paragraph extends beyond, say, two-thirds of a page, it should probably be broken into two.

Lengthy paragraphs can also be a sign, incidentally, of exactly the opposite problem: summary. This occurs when an author tells far too much and does not show enough, presenting the action secondhand. Reading too much summary is like having someone tell you at length about his hot date—hearing about such a date is not nearly as much fun as living one!

Perhaps one of the easiest ways to judge the pacing of your own writing is to note the *balance* of dialogue and narrative. In contemporary prose, authors tend to write in scenes, which are portrayed in both exposition and conversation. "Balance" doesn't mean, in terms of space allotted to each, a fifty-fifty split. Nonetheless, large chunks in which nobody says a word and page after page of all talk are signs of imbalance. Jorge Luis Borges wrote various masterpieces of short prose with not a single word between quotation marks, whereas an author such as Mary Robison can produce achingly real stories with the absolute minimum of narration. Most writers and the stories they tell, however, fall somewhere between these two extremes.

TRANSITIONS

Pace and balance are often influenced by another issue in prose—transitions. Apprentice writers sometimes have trouble moving from scene to scene in a story and in the process of trying they include action and dialogue that is extraneous to their tales.

As Part I mentioned the use of white space, the "enter" key is your friend for many transitional instances. Assuming you think in scenes, you can easily shift from one to the next by double-spacing twice. This has no intrinsic significance; it merely cues the reader that, in the text that follows, something changes. The story might progress from a different point of view or location. Maybe the action picks up at a later time or even at an earlier time.

White space is extremely useful, but—here we go again—don't overdo it. Too much white space can cut up a text and make for a jerky read. Beyond that, it can confuse the reader if you have, for example, consistently used it to signify a shift in time and then you suddenly employ it to indicate a new point of view. White space can also make a writer look lazy; a writer can use it as a crutch to avoid composing a line or paragraph that would move the text more smoothly from one scene to another.

The trick with transitions is to find a happy medium. In our anxiousness about losing or confusing the reader, we may tend to overexplain and feature a lot of unnecessary dialogue, description, action, and so on, that, in the end, simply bores the audience as they wonder why they're being subjected to so much trivial information.

That's what happens with the following passage:

"Catch you later, Brad!"

Lynette picked up her purse and headed out the door. She half skipped across the lawn and opened the door of her green '99 Pontiac Grand Am, and headed for her mother's house. She turned left at Mountain Boulevard and drove the three miles to Upland Street. Traffic was awful: stop and go, stop and go. She opened her purse and unwrapped the Hershey bar she'd bought earlier at CVS. It took her ten minutes longer than usual to make the trip, and her mood had darkened considerably.

"So, what is it this time, Ma?" she said crossly as she banged through the screen door.

There's nothing mechanically wrong with this text, but the reader has to ask, "Is anything revealed here significant?" The color, make, and model of Lynette's car; the names of local streets; the Hershey bar—do we need to know any of this? We might, but, unless these details have some larger meaning in the story, it's probably best to eliminate them.

"Catch you later, Brad!"

Lynette picked up her purse and headed out the door.

Traffic was awful, and, by the time she reached her mother's, her mood had darkened considerably.

"So, what is it this time, Ma?" she said crossly as she banged through the screen door.

Overelaborate transitions are something even experienced writers produce. Many experienced authors include in their early drafts passages that are finally extraneous to their stories. This isn't a problem for writers who recognize that quality about those passages. Indeed, as the action unfolds before the author, the actual production of such sentences or paragraphs may be absolutely necessary. As we have noted many times before, when we write, we tell ourselves the story for the first time, and we may include information that we as authors need to know but the readers don't. For example, it may be useful for the writer to work out early on in the text the route Lynette follows to get from Brad's house to her mother's, though this will not be important until later in the story. The elimination of these extraneous elements happens later, during editing and revising of a text.

These transitional moments often represent "dead time." Nothing of real import is happening: For example, a character is driving someplace or taking a shower or sleeping or making pasta. Readers don't need to go step-by-step through these processes, so such moments are often excellent opportunities for writers to provide further information about a character—her history, her plans, and so on. Indeed, in life, people reflect on the past or consider the future when they are engaged in these quotidian activities. The following uses Lynette's drive as such an opportunity.

"Catch you later, Brad!"

Lynette picked up her purse and headed out the door.

Traffic was awful, and as it crawled along—stop and go, stop and go—Lynette grew more and more irritated. Her mother was always doing this to her. She had actually enjoyed watching the game with Brad. She might never be a true baseball fan, but seeing his boyish excitement as his beloved Red Sox took the lead in the fifth inning gave her access to part of him she had never really seen before.

Then the phone rang, and she was, as Willie Nelson put it, on the road again.

Even when she was a little girl, it was the same. She might be playing with her dolls when she was seven, out for a last round of tag in the after-dinner twilight at eleven, chatting with Tymika or Brenda about what a hunk that new boy, Frankie, was at fifteen—and then she would hear that quavering whine: *Lynette. Lynette, honey. Can you come here?*

And Lynette would go to her. *Set the table. Dry the dishes. Can you help me look for that green scarf, the one your Aunt Lana gave me?* Her mother was not mean to her. It was simply that she needed attention, constant attention, and, with only the two of them there, who else could the woman turn to?

Lynette wondered how different things might have been if her father had not taken off and taken Larry with him when she was only three.

By the time she reached her mother's, her mood had darkened considerably.

"So, what is it this time, Ma?" she said crossly as she banged through the screen door.

The hiatus in the story's action has been exploited. The drive from Brad's to Lynette's mother's house is a trivial action, but Lynette's thoughts during the trip are not trivial at all. During this dead time, readers gain a great deal of insight into Lynette's upbringing, family situation, and life. Readers learn that her parents split up when she was three; she has a brother named Larry, who she probably doesn't know very well; and her mother is not a cruel woman, but a lonely one who needs and has always needed someone to pay attention to her.

And, for a very long time, that someone has been Lynette.

As you shift from scene to scene, vary your technique. For example, within the confines of a short story or a chapter, employ white space in a consistent way—that is, to signal a particular kind of shift, as in time, place, or point of view—then, elsewhere, use dead time to elaborate on a character or setting. Interlacing significant information within the context of the central action generally allows you to transmit it more succinctly than straight chronological narrative does. These moments can add a great deal of richness to your text and, interestingly enough, make it tighter and shorter.

19

Accuracy

Despite that old chesnut of creative writing courses, "Write what you know," many times writers prefer to write about something they have little knowledge of. This is great, but—in most circumstances, anyway—that doesn't get authors off the hook where the verisimilitude of their creations are concerned. Should you decide to introduce characters who are very different from you, whether by ethnicity or religion or historical moment, or to set a story in a place or time that is not your own, that's fine, but you will have to do a certain amount of research to assure that your invention is convincing for your audience.

While this may seem self-evident, the question "Does it have to be accurate?" comes up in workshops with astonishing frequency. Off the top of my head, I can remember many apprentice stories that went off the track because the writers failed to look at a map or verify when a particular invention first became generally available or a public health problem first emerged. One author had a drug-addicted character die of AIDS in 1972. From what we know of the disease's history, that is plausible. The problem, however, is that in 1972 we did not yet know that such a malady existed, much less know what to call it. It was a decade later, when AIDS began to manifest itself with alarming frequency in New York and San Francisco, before the syndrome was identified and named.

GEOGRAPHY

Most problems with accuracy occur in three categories: geography, history, and specialized knowledge. Accuracy in geography applies equally to real places (as you might expect) and fictional places (which you might not). If you decide to set a story in New York City or Singapore or the Everglades, it is incumbent upon you to familiarize yourself with that place unless you already have first-hand knowledge of it. You can't have a character get off the PATH train from New Jersey at Grand Central Station, which is at Forty-second Street and Park Avenue on the East Side, simply because the PATH's tunnels terminate at Pennsylvania Station, which lies on the West Side between Thirty-first and Thirty-third Streets and faces the Avenue of the Americas. Further, if you write about New York City in the years before World War II, you call the avenue in question Sixth Avenue. Indeed, if you imitate a New Yorker, you would still call it Sixth Avenue simply because, despite Gotham's fathers' best efforts, those who live there, with perhaps typical cussedness, have never adopted the name change.

So, what to do? The most attractive option might be to spend a month in New York—or Singapore or Florida. The problem with that, sad to say, is that the vast majority of writers don't have the cash or leisure time on hand to jump on a plane for a four-week stay in the locale of our choice, even in the name of research.

For considerably less money, however, you can choose from a number of alternatives. Buy a map; get a good guidebook. You may not even have to cough up any cash. The Internet provides numerous resources you can consult for free. Beyond this, read a few contemporary novels set in the city; look at collections of photographs; and pick up some copies of *The New York Times*, the *New York Post*, or the *Daily News*. If your action transpires at the World's Fair of 1939, then hit your local library or used book store to seek out the texts that would have been around at the twilight of the Depression. Over the years, I've had occasion to consult the state guidebooks produced by the Work Projects Administration during the Franklin Roosevelt years; these books are a gold mine of information about what any one of the lower forty-eight was like in the first third of the Twentieth Century. Remember that places—man-made ones anyway—are "living" entities: They change over time. Evoking the New York of 1939 is different than evoking the New York of 2002. Even if the street grid was essentially the same then as it is now, what faces those streets, the characters of various neighborhoods, and the kind of vendors that populate the sidewalks have changed.

In recent years, reference texts that specialize in helping writers establish their settings accurately have become available and might prove useful to you, particularly if, in your story, you need only general notions of a city's layout.

Even if you later need to go into greater detail, such a volume might give you enough information to get through your first draft, where you concentrate on your plot and characters. Filling in from more-detailed sources the needed "color" of the setting can come later.

When you invent a city or town, you have more freedom to mould things as you see fit. Even so, except perhaps in science fiction and fantasy, there are limits on the liberties you can take. Faulkner's Yoknapatawpha County does not really exist, yet readers know that it is located in Mississippi; as a consequence, it's unlikely readers would have accepted the notion of the town of Jefferson falling victim to a sudden blizzard. Faulkner based his fictional place on one he knew well—the town of Oxford in Jefferson County, where there is, as it happens, a Yoknapatawpha Creek. Still, even if your locale is not strictly based upon a real one, you are constrained by logic—the realities of ecology and geology and so on. Several years back, I had a student who presented a very rough draft of a novel, and, during discussion in the workshop, his fellows expressed some perplexity about the topography described in the manuscript. At one point, he wrote of a butte looming over the small town; later, he evoked leafy glens and green hills. The author explained, in all innocence, that he had not yet decided whether his story transpired in West Virginia or Wyoming.

Such a decision is not a minor one. The simple fact is that the terrain, the flora, and the fauna of a state smack in the middle of the Appalachian Mountains are significantly different from those in the arid vastness of a state traversed by the Rockies. Even if he never intended to identify the specific region where his fictional town was located, he, as the writer, needed to know where it was. Setting, after all, is one of the essential elements in any story. A reader wants to be able to conceive of your characters within a context, within their world. You can go overboard on this, spending so much time meticulously describing every detail of little Sammy Villar's barrio that your audience feels they've been trapped in some photo-essay mysteriously rendered in words. However, beyond the issue of too much detail vs. not enough, make sure the details you do provide are consistent.

Geographic accuracy can be a particularly acute problem for those writing autobiographical fiction or memoirs. Unlike in more intensely fictional narrative, here the author already knows the places intimately. She knows what her girlhood bedroom looked like and what flowers were in bloom in May, so she may tend to "underwrite" the actual physical reality of the space her characters inhabit, as well as the the characters themselves.

Before those who write science fiction and fantasy breathe a sigh of relief, remember that, even in these genres, the world in which your tale is set presumably has a climate, a topography, a way of measuring time, and so on, and those need to be written consistently within that particular place. While you could invent a realm in which absolutely everything constantly shape-shifts, this would likely prove challenging to read and cause attention to focus on the ongoing changes rather than characters or plot. Samuel Delany in his Nevèryon novels or Doris Lessing in her *Golden Notebook* must constantly recall the climates and landscapes of the worlds they have made.

HISTORY

If your story is set in the past, familiarize yourself with what that past was like. For example, if your setting is Raleigh, North Carolina, during World War II, you need to know that this was a segregated town, it had streetcars and blackout drills, and in it, items from meat to gasoline were rationed. Your characters might have a "party line"—a single telephone line that serves various residences—so the phone will ring differently depending on who on the line is being called, and a character might well pick up the phone only to discover it is already in use. Character's travel beyond Raleigh will be largely by train. There will be no television. The war will be a constant, haunting presence in virtually everybody's lives.

Again, the key here is research, though you needn't become an expert on conditions on the homefront from 1941 to 1945 to write your story. In the library, you should be able to find a number of good general texts, both nonfiction and fiction, describing what life was like during the period. There is also a significant filmography of movies made during the war or afterward. Beyond this, look at newspapers and magazines of the era—*Newsweek, Life, Better Homes and Gardens, The Atlantic Monthly*, and so on. Pay attention to not only the news articles, the editorials, and the fiction, but also the advertising. What did people wear, read, and dream of? Where did they vacation? Who endorsed products? These details can give you a real feel for your characters' time and allow you to make it real for your audience.

If you deal with twentieth-century events you can consult a population of informants—your grandmother, your uncle, the nice old lady down the street, maybe even your great-grandfather. People's concrete memories of a particular period can provide you with details great and small that lend texture to your evocation of it. People found ways to get around rationing, trading coupons back and forth depending on their wants and needs, and some found ways (as people always do) to get a little more than their fair share of coffee or tires or beef. Despite the ongoing horrors of wartime periods, people still fell in love, had sex, reared children, went to the opera, played bridge, got drunk, gossiped, and fought and made up. These are the kinds of tidbits that you might not find in publications. If you acquire far more information than you ultimately can use in your tale, all the better. You will have a larger sense of your story's time frame and be able to confidently bring it to life on the page.

In certain instances the appearance of an anachronism or some other absurd element works. It's fun to imagine an ancient Greece with motor scooters or an Incan empire in which Atahualpa plays boccie ball with Pizarro. This can be a wonderful way to satirize our contemporary style of living. Mark Twain had a great time with this sort of thing in *A Connecticut Yankee in King Arthur's Court*, which is much more about post–Civil War America than it is about Camelot. Nonetheless, Twain steeped himself in Arthurian lore, likely following the development of Alfred Lord Tennyson's *Idylls of the King*, a serious epic poem published in parts between 1859 and 1885. For all the fun Twain had, he gets his knights and legendary events right, even if they are skewed by the arrival of the nineteenth-century visitor.

The need for such care by writers who deal with alternative histories is well illustrated by such novels as Philip K. Dick's *The Man in the High Castle* or Robert Harris's *Fatherland*, both of which deal with a world in which Imperial Japan and the Third Reich triumphed in World War II. These men knew their Nazis: Dick spent seven years researching his book; Harris is the author of *Selling Hitler*. To cite another example, William Gibson and Bruce Sterling imagine in *The Difference Engine* a Victorian age in which the computer has already been invented (albeit powered by steam). The 1855 London they evoke, however, though obviously different from the one that actually existed, suffers from the class divisions and pollution and blight and hunger that propelled the novels of Dickens.

SPECIALIZED KNOWLEDGE

Finally, accuracy is essential in any fiction that demands a degree of specialized knowledge. If you write a story about miners, you should know at least a little about mining; prisoners, what prison life is like; making a cake, baking. Years back, a young man in a class of mine attempted to describe a woman putting on her makeup, and he was informed that "anybody who put on mascara like that would put her eye out." Likewise, more recently, a student writing about baseball brought down upon her head the wrath of all the Tigers fans—both male and female—in the workshop, who were incensed at her ignorance of the finer points of bunting and base stealing.

This issue is most prominent in connection with genre fiction—mystery, thriller, police procedural, military yarn, courtroom drama, and so on. I once had a student who was attempting to write a story about a big-city murder. As it happened, another student in the class had spent a number of years as a reporter on the city desk of the *Chicago Tribune*. Each time a new episode of the mystery came in, the former reporter would blast away at the conduct of the police and their mode of investigation: "The officer just contaminated the evidence . . . couldn't ask the suspect that . . . made sure the case would be thrown out of court!" The problem was that the author really had no idea of precisely how those in law enforcement go about trying to solve a crime or what strictures they operate under in their legal pursuit of a solution.

If you plan to write about cops or lawyers or private investigators or soldiers, you need to know how the realms in which they operate are structured. Who reports to whom? How easily can rules be bent or broken? What can legitimately be viewed, for example, as incriminating evidence? Once again, it is not difficult to learn about these things, but be careful of what sources you employ. *Perry Mason*, in which our hero always defends innocents and has astonishing luck in wringing courtroom confessions from the real perpetrators, does not exactly provide a true sense of how the law works. Even more contemporary series, for a variety of reasons, still play pretty fast and loose with investigative and legal realities. A better bet for a model might be true crime books and journalistic descriptions of particular crimes.

Further, you can always have your story vetted by someone who actually works in the field you write about. These "advisors" can be friends, acquaintances, or strangers. You might pay someone to be your consultant, though many people are willing to read such a text free of charge. Veterans at the local American Legion can provide you with battlefield lore you won't find in the history books, and a cop on the beat can let you in on some stories where procedures are followed to the letter and others where their spirit, at least, is violated.

Of course, you always have the library and the Internet. The latter, admittedly, may require a certain amount of skill or experience. The search engines available are fabulous, but you do need to know how to specify your topic so that you don't end up with 845,247 hits. Your best bet is to gradually narrow your search ("World War II," then "Italian Campaign," then "Anzio," then "Mark Clark") as you move from Web site to Web site. The library is easier in the sense that you can see what's available laid out before you. And, in major facilities, you really should get to know the reference librarian, who can be extremely helpful in putting you onto the right sources and may himself be imbued with a remarkable curiosity that drives him to go to great lengths to help you find the information you need.

* * *

So, why do all this? The reason to go to this trouble is simple: As an author, the last thing you want is to commit some howling error that will instantly disrupt your reader's connection with the text. You, the writer, enter into an implicit contract with your reader to provide a text that honestly evokes the story's world.

20

Allusions

Many times when we write, we make reference to things existing outside the story. These things can be highly contemporary (a popular song or film, a hip saying, a celebrity, a news event) or more traditional (a noted play or other literary work, a Bible story, a historical figure, a famous battle). Both of these kinds of **allusion** can add texture and richness to a story, but they can be tricky.

TOPICAL ALLUSION

The first type, a **topical allusion**, can, over time, simply lose its meaning or make a situation or character seem merely quaint. In 2000, the expression "go postal," in the sense of committing sudden random acts of senseless violence, probably still resonates with most people, who recall a series of highly publicized shootings involving employees of the U.S. Postal Service in the 1980s and early 1990s. However, twenty years from now, this expression may be completely opaque to most readers.

If I were to have a character say, "Yeah, Robbie made a regular Checkers speech," how many readers under forty would know that this referred to a once famous television address by Richard Nixon during the 1952 presidential campaign? Accused of accepting gifts as the Republican nominee for vice-president, Nixon denied any improprieties and closed his presentation by mentioning a puppy that had been given to his daughters and, he affirmed, would not be returned to the original owner. "The Checkers speech" became shorthand for a sentimental pull at the public's heartstrings. It's quite possible, however, that those born after, say, 1965 would have absolutely no idea what was being referred to.

Thirty years ago, in the age of just three television networks and Top 40 radio stations, a time when talking film was less than fifty years old, an author could assume that some allusions to the popular culture would be generally understood throughout the society. People would know who James Cagney was and who The Supremes were, they would know the source of the expression "Sock it to me," and they would be aware that the coterie surrounding Frank Sinatra was referred to as "The Rat Pack."

Such general understanding is no longer a given. Audiences have atomized, with some people listening only to techno or heavy metal or Christian rock. Cable and satellite television offer literally hundreds of channels. Tens of thousands of American films are extant, and, if you factor in those from Europe, Latin America, India, and so on, the number becomes astronomical.

Creating effective allusion can be difficult now even with established cultural artifacts. Melville's initial audience was cued from the first line of *Moby Dick* that this would be a story of wandering of some sort because of the Biblical story of Ishmael: the son of Abraham and his concubine, Hagar; the half brother of Isaac; and the purported ancestor of the nomadic Bedouins. Likewise, almost one hundred years later, Faulkner could still assume a general store of shared knowledge among his readers, including an awareness of who Absalom was or where "sound and fury" came from (King David's rebellious son, by the way, and Shakespeare's *Macbeth*). With changes in education and the explosion of information available, however, this is no longer the case.

APPROPRIATE ALLUSION

Also to be considered is the appropriateness of the allusions writers employ. This can be a subtle matter, especially as the allusions grow more complex and interdependent. For example, I recently read a memoir in progress in which the author frequently referenced the films, television programs, and screen celebrities of his childhood and youth. This was perfectly reasonable because, in the bumpy, working-class world in which he grew up, these larger-than-life fantasies and personalities provided a certain stability as well as a glimpse into lives very different from his own.

Things got shaky, however, when the allusions arrived weighted with elements the writer did not intend or with resonances that seemed out of synch with the character or situation to which the allusion applied. In one instance, the boy is delivered unto the decidedly Dickensian mercies of his maternal grandparents. His grandfather, in particular, is presented as a first-class ogre— a terrifying figure for the five-year-old protagonist. At one point, the grandfather is described as wearing sleeveless undershirts, "like Stanley Kowalski in *A Streetcar Named Desire*." Later on, when the child is beaten for not eating his dinner, the author compares the experience of anticipating the grandfather's blows to watching the renowned "shower scene" in Alfred Hitchcock's *Psycho*, and makes reference to the grandfather as "Norman Bates."

What's problematic here is that, in both these instances, the allusions come freighted with elements not entirely in accord with the evoked experience itself. Tennessee Williams's Kowalski—brutish though he may be— was portrayed on both stage and screen by the young Marlon Brando. Indeed, for the actor, the role was career making, establishing him as an icon of intensely male sexuality, a kind of gritty "pinup boy" in the age of the gray flannel suit. Kowalski's is not an admirable role in Williams's play, but his character is more finely shaded and complex than the memoir's allusion allows for.

The inclusion of the Norman Bates reference is even more debatable. The twitchy, Oedipally fixated killer brought to life by Anthony Perkins is terrifying, at least in part, because he is superficially so mild mannered and unthreatening, just the opposite of the mean-tempered and violent grandfather in the memoir. And yet, of course, Norman Bates is ultimately far more deadly because he is literally psychotic. The allusion's problem in the scene of the beating is compounded because, during the assault, the child insists that he is "a good boy" and cries out for both his mother and his father, which arguably links the boy, not the marauding old man, to Bates.

While a passing reference to both of the two films may have been useful, the reinforcement of these images weighs down the text with all kinds of inappropriate baggage. The grandfather is mean and loutish, entirely unsympathetic. He is not young and attractive like Kowalski, nor is he endowed with Kowalski's intense, virile magnetism that both fascinates and repels Blanche DuBois. Nor is the grandfather possessed of the youth, apparent meekness, or real madness of Norman Bates. The elaborate allusions to both figures muddy the waters, raising ambiguities and introducing elements of sexuality that are simply inappropriate in the context of the boy's unjust punishment.

CLARITY OF ALLUSION

Avoid being needlessly obscure in your allusions. Not long ago, a workshop member evoked in his story the final scene of Pierre Boulle's novel, *Planet of the Apes*, or, to put it more accurately, the final scene of the film from the 1960s movie based upon Boulle's book. Therein, protagonist Charlton Heston—having fled the civilization established by the various gorillas, chimps, orangutans, and so on, and located on what he has assumed to be a planet far, far away—stumbles upon the shattered remains of the Statue of Liberty. He then realizes that rather than having come to rest in some distant galaxy, his spacecraft has accidentally tumbled back to Earth, which, in his extended absence, has been blown to smithereens by his human cousins and delivered unto the apes.

Alluding to the film would have been fine, except that the writer never actually mentions the title of the movie or the ruin that Heston confronts. As it turns out, the image of the Statue of Liberty plays a significant role in the story. Hence, if the reader is unfamiliar with the novel or film, she either has no notion at all of what was subsequently going on or has to parse it out painstakingly on her own. The author had no problem with that. He felt that the reader should feel obligated to seek out the information necessary to understand the allusion, as he himself had done many times when studying great works of literature.

This is okay—up to a point. Certainly, when we sit down with some canonical novel (James Joyce's *Ulysses*, let's say, or Hemingway's *For Whom the Bell Tolls*), we anticipate (more in the former than the latter, perhaps) that we may have to investigate some things in order to comprehend all the various facets of the text. However, we are likely studying these books either as part of a fiction course or because we feel we should be familiar with them. Readers are a lot more likely to invest time and effort in capturing all the nuances of the work of a writer they have been told is sacrosanct than in that of a writer whose name is, as yet anyway, not one to conjure with.

Further, as best I could tell anyway, there was no compelling reason in this particular story for *Planet of the Apes*'s Statue of Liberty not to be identified outright. It is certainly possible to employ an allusion that remains thickly veiled, as in a story in which the final significance of a parallel to a famous text is to be revealed only at the end (though this does carry a considerable risk of the work appearing merely gimmicky, keeping from the reader key information and springing it upon her at the last minute like the punch line of a joke).

Of course, in politically repressive cultures, the veiled allusion is a time-honored means of criticizing the dominant culture without getting caught, in that censors (thank God!) tend toward being astonishingly literal minded. Aleksandr Solzhenitsyn's *Cancer Ward* was obviously a metaphor on a variety of levels for a different disease—the Soviet system itself—that the author saw as consuming, body and soul, the Russia he loved, and yet this book was published in the Soviet Union.

I encountered another example of this when I was in Argentina in the 1970s. With the country in the grip of a brutal military government, a film directed by Mario Sábato appeared and was based on a section of the novel *Regarding Heros and Tombs* by his father, Ernesto Sábato. This largely self-contained narrative is called *Report Regarding the Blind,* which Sábato the Younger turned into a movie called *The Power of Darkness.* The story concerns a man's growing understanding of and terror at an immense, apocalyptic conspiracy among the blind people of Buenos Aires. What is amazing is that the military censors failed to see that the entire situation could be read, in the 1970s, as a parallel to the current climate in Argentina, with its omnipresent secret police, its clandestine prisons and torture chambers, its ugly habit of "disappearing" people the government had determined were some somehow "subversive" or "enemies of The National Process." The film played to capacity crowds in 1979, and everyone I spoke to about it seemed to find the movie's allusion to the contemporary circumstances utterly transparent.

BLATANT ALLUSION

Just as you can be too obscure in your allusions, you can also be too overt. Try naming a character Polonius, for example, or Judas. More frequent even than that kind of ham-handedness are instances where an author yields to the temptation to "overexplain" an allusion to make sure that the audience gets it. Here is an example.

> "Frankly, my dear, I don't give a damn," he said in his best Clark Gable imitation, looking as insouciant as Rhett Butler.

Okay! Okay! We get it! Don't be afraid to count on your audience's familiarity with either Margaret Mitchell's *Gone With the Wind* or David Selznik's film production of it. You might get away with mentioning either the fictional hero or the actor who portrayed him, but the two together bludgeon the reader about the head. Too, a reader who does not catch your drift from the quotation itself and still fails to catch it when you toss out Gable's name is not going to get it when you bring up Butler. For that reader, the allusion is simply lost.

You can cue your audience to what you're referencing without insulting them. Sad to say, if you write

Ralph was ready for his transformation into a teenage Fagin.

Some readers will not immediately pick up on the analogy between Ralph and Fagin, Charles Dickens's brilliantly realized organizer of a ring of boy thieves in 1840s London. Let's say you elaborate a bit on the allusion.

Ralph was ready for his transformation into a teenage Fagin, and Eddie was the obvious candidate to play the Artful Dodger.

It's a nice image, but, if the reader isn't clear on who Fagin is, the mention of another member of the ring is probably not going to help. However, the name of one other character might at least point the audience to what you're talking about. Let's take a third run at this.

Ralph was ready for his transformation into a teenage Fagin, and Eddie was the obvious candidate to play the Artful Dodger. The only question was who in the gang would be Oliver Twist.

At this point, as they say in the musical *Oklahoma*, you've gone "about as 'fur' as you can go." You've provided, without too much ado, the title of the novel in which Fagin and the Artful Dodger appear, which happens to be the name of its central character. If your reader is competely at sea when it comes to the novels of Charles Dickens, that's the end of this, and the allusion will be lost on her. However, a considerable percentage of your audience, even if they haven't actually read *Oliver Twist*, will have seen the musical or a film based on it, have perused the book's *Cliff's Notes* back in high school, or at least have heard somebody talk about the story.

* * *

Allusion to the wider world, to other texts, to art, and so on, can add a great deal of resonance to a story. In this day and age, however, allusion should perhaps be employed sparingly, not necessarily as an essential element in a text. For the reader who understands an allusion, the text has greater depth and soul. To accommodate the one who doesn't get it, however, writers should be sure that comprehension of the allusion is not absolutely necessary to understanding the story.

21

Experimentation and the Avant-Garde

For the last couple hundred years at least, writers and most other creative types have liked to think of themselves as being "on the cutting edge" of the culture in which we live, boldly going, to update the *Star Trek* credo, where no man or woman has gone before. Especially in the last century or so, about the worst thing you could say about any piece of prose or other art was that it was "old-fashioned." To be "avant-garde"—in French, literally part of the "advance guard"—seemed ipso facto virtuous. As Ezra Pound exhorted us all at the beginning of the Twentieth Century, "Make it new!"

This has not always been the case. Thanks to archeology, we know that humanity passed through stone ages, a bronze age, an iron age, and so on, but the ancients and those who came after them, up until the Romantic Era of the Nineteenth Century, saw humanity not as "evolving" but "devolving." We were becoming, by definition, less virtuous than our ancestors, pulling ever farther away from a Golden Age when all was right with the world. This idea in Greek and Hellenistic philosophy was a powerful one. In the Judeo-Christian tradition, it found a perfect analogue in the notion that, after the fall from grace of Adam and Eve and their expulsion from Eden, we were even further from the initial innocence of creation and deeply mired in the sin and death of the material world.

Hence, for most of human history, rather than creating something new, writers looked to replicate the finer works of old. It is no accident that Dante's guide through Hell and Purgatory is the Roman poet Virgil, author of the *Aeneid*, an epic poem that itself intended to imitate the epic poems of the Greeks, especially Homer's *Iliad* and *Odyssey*. John Milton, in his Protestant epics, essentially tried to do the same thing. *Paradise Lost* was meant to give to the new, dissident

Christian literature the same cachet as that the Classical poets had given to their civilizations. Even the Elizabethan and Jacobean playwrights—remarkably innovative writers—operated under the shadow of their ancient forebears. Ben Jonson, in his *Sejanus*, tried to bring to the contemporary stage the kind of tragedy the Roman Seneca had brought to his, and there was a circle surrounding the Countess of Pembroke who were attempting to do the same thing—in Latin, no less. The French Neoclassical writers such as Racine and Corneille, having discovered what they considered to be the unities of time, place, and action, pursued the same goal.

On one hand, we can be happy that a taste for innovation has come to characterize not merely literature, but all writing and most other aspects of our lives. At the same time, remember that innovation in and of itself can often result in mere cleverness or lead to nothing more than a dead end. The previous century is littered with brave artistic movements, complete with ringing manifestos and rife with wild experimentation, that never took us much of anywhere. Instead of revolutionizing art as we know it, at best they expanded the boundaries a bit of what we perceive as art. They let us look at fiction or painting or poetry in a new way, and so they enriched the palette of devices and designs available to us creative types as we went about our work.

The point here is to encourage you to keep "experimentation" in perspective. There's nothing wrong with deviating from the conventions we've discussed in this book; before you do so, just remember to establish exactly what you're trying to accomplish. When e.e. cummings threw the rules of capitalization out the window in his poetry, it looked wildly new. When we do it, we look more like we're imitating e.e. cummings. In *Another Country*, had James Baldwin had his character Rufus think of himself as a lowercase "i" as he journeyed toward jumping off the George Washington Bridge, we would likely have read this as a mere rip-off of Faulkner's *The Sound and the Fury*, in which Quentin does precisely that when on his way to throw himself off the Harvard Bridge over the Charles River in Cambridge, Massachusetts.

There are times when violating the conventions is perfectly acceptable. In my own novel *Mrs. Randall*, I wanted a concluding moment in the book in which two characters simultaneously misidentify one another and hence misinterpret the significance of sighting each other, so I wrote them in two columns. The copyeditor then made them sequential, and I screamed bloody murder. With my editor's support, we kept the columns.

Nonetheless, remember always your audience! Whom do you want as your readers? Who will read and appreciate your work? If you write for a small coterie or if you are convinced that in fifty years, your innovation will have become part of the writer's standard toolbox, then have at it. Do recall, though, that these peculiarities

- can alienate some readers
- tend to draw attention to themselves
- can break the implicit imaginative contract between reader and writer

As a result, readers may think of the world you create on the page in terms of a text or an artifice. They will deal with your story, your world, more intellectually than emotionally and fail to become immersed in it. Further, with the passage of time, your remarkable innovation may end up looking merely peculiar or (even worse!) rather quaint.

William Gass, certainly no stick-in-the-mud himself as a writer, sets the bar pretty high when it comes to justifying our innovations.

Most newness is new in all the same old ways: Falsely, as products are said to be new by virtue of minuscule and trivial additions; or vapidly, when the touted differences are pointless; or opportunistically, when alterations are made simply in order to profit from imaginary improvements; or differentially, when newness merely marks a moment, place, or person off from others and gives it its own identity, however dopey.

If your experiment in prose escapes the rubrics Gass sets forth, then you're onto something.

INDEX